Girl Talk with God

Girl Talk with God

SUSIE SHELLENBERGER

W PUBLISHING GROUP™

www.wpublishinggroup.com

A Division of Thomas Nelson, Inc.
www.ThomasNelson.com

Published by W Publishing Group, a division of Thomas Nelson Company,
P.O. Box 141000, Nashville, Tennessee, 37214, in association with the literary agency of
Alive Communications, Inc., 7680 Goddard Street, Suite 200,
Colorado Springs, Colorado, 80920.

Library of Congress Cataloging-in-Publication Data

Shellenberger, Susie.
    Girl talk with God / Susie Shellenberger.
        p. cm.
    ISBN 0-8499-4290-X
    1. Teenage girls—Religious life. 2. Imaginary conversations. 3. Christian life. I. Title.

BV4551.3 .S54 2001   2001035898
248.8'33—dc21

Printed in the United States of America

04 05 06 PHX 0 9 8

Dedicated to Gaye Marston, whose ministry
and prayers reach far outside Fredricksburg, Virginia.
Thank you for loving teen girls and investing your life
into their well-being through professional counseling.
You're the best!

Table of Contents

Acknowledgments

The following chapters of the present work appeared in a slightly different version in the following sources and are reprinted with permission of the publishers:

Chapter 4, "On God's Love," published in *Brio* magazine (February 1999); Chapter 5, "On Hypocrisy," published in *Brio* magazine (December 1998); Chapter 6, "On Spending Time with God," published in *Brio* magazine (May 1999); Chapter 7, "On Boyfriends," published in *Brio* magazine (September 1999); Chapter 8, "On Language," published in *Brio* magazine (April 1996); Chapter 9, "On Hell," published in *Keeping Your Cool While Sharing Your Faith*, by Greg Johnson and Susie Shellenberger (Wheaton, Ill.: Tyndale, 1993); Chapter 11, "On Forgiveness," published in *Help! My Friend's in Trouble*, by Susie Shellenberger (Ann Arbor, Mich.: Servant, 2000); Chapter 12, "On Reaching Out," published in *Help! My Friend's in Trouble*, by Susie Shellenberger (Ann Arbor, Mich.: Servant, 2000); Chapter 13, "On Sex," published in *The Mother/Daughter Connection* (Nashville, Word, 2000).

Read This First!

I'm glad you picked up this book. Know what I do when I pick up a new book? *I smell it!* Te-hee. (Our little secret, okay?) It's true. I love the smell of new books . . . and the inside of new tennis shoes, and hot dogs sizzling on the grill, and fresh-cut roses . . . and a bunch of other scents I won't take the time to bore you with.

But you're not the only one who knows my favorite smells. God knows them too. Yep, it's true. I tell Him all the things I love to smell. (I tell Him a lot of other stuff too.) I absolutely love talking to Jesus. And the most exciting part? It's when He talks back!

That's right. God and I have conversations. A lot of them.

Do you have conversations with God? The fancy name for it is *prayer.* That may sound a little high and lofty, but it's actually all about talking to Him and listening to Him talk back.

If you're having trouble praying, think of prayer as a conversation—a really intimate conversation with the Creator of the universe. You can tell Him anything. I'm serious! And the cool part? He'll never laugh. He'll always understand. And He loves nothing better than having conversations with you. It's true!

Maybe some of these conversations will spark some of your own. Start writing them down if you want. You'll be surprised at the difference conversations with the King of Kings can make. I promise!

Your Friend,
Susie Shellenberger

On Becoming a Christian

*D*o you realize that most of the people in America consider themselves to be Christians? Yet many would also admit they don't have a personal, growing relationship with Jesus Christ. They consider themselves Christians, however, because they assume a Christian is someone who believes in God and tries to be a good person.

You probably have friends and teachers at school who have bought into this assumption. It's tragic to realize they believe a lie. The Bible is crystal-clear on what being a Christian is. And it's much more than simply acknowledging with our brain that there's a God.

Following Jesus Christ affects every single area of our lives. It requires a lifestyle change. But the rewards are beyond description. After all, who among us deserves forgiveness for sins? The beautiful, exciting thing about Christianity is realizing that we'll never be good enough for God but He loves and accepts us anyway. We'll never deserve His forgiveness and the gift of eternal life, yet He offers them freely.

As you read this first conversation between a teen girl and God, search your own heart and make sure you're not merely professing with your lips and not living the life with your heart and actions.

God said: How was church?
I said: Fine. I guess.
Were you listening?
Yeah. Sure.
What was the sermon about?
Oh, You know. Being a Christian—that stuff.
Ever thought about taking it to heart?
I'm clueless, God.
That's what saddens Me.
Are You trying to tell me something?
Sure am.
Okay. What's on Your heart?
It's what's *not* in yours.
'Scuze me?

Me. I'm not in your heart. But I sure would like to be.

Funny, God. Real funny. Of course You are. We're hanging.

No. I'm talking about being a Christian.

I *am* a Christian!

No, My child. You're not.

Sure I am!

What *is* a Christian?

Someone who believes in You.

Hm. Satan believes in Me.

Well . . . yeah, but—

Is he a Christian?

Of course not!

So, a Christian isn't simply someone who believes in Me.

Huh. Never thought about that.

Back to the question: What *is* a Christian?

A good person.

Is *anyone* good? All of mankind was born with sin.

Well, You know. A Christian is someone who does good things.

So all Boy Scouts are Christians?

Sigh. No. Come on, God. This is frustrating. You know what I mean.

I need you to verbalize it.

Okay. Being a Christian is doing good things and going to church. Oh, and reading the Bible—that's important.

My child, are you aware that numerous religion classes are taught in universities around the world? Many of them study Christianity—along with other religions—and those students are required to read the Bible. If those students try real hard to do good things, read the Bible as part of their class requirements, and go to church—to write a report about it—would they be classified as Christians?

Oh, man! I hate this, God. You're gettin' all deep on me. Can we quit being so religious and just cut to the chase?

Good point. Because Christianity isn't a religion.

Sure it is!

No, My child. Christianity isn't a religion—it's a way of life.

Well . . .

And I'd like to make it *your* way of life.

I so don't get You, God. I'm already a Christian. Why are You after me? Go after a thief or a murderer or a porn publisher.

Why? You're in the same boat they're in.

What?!?!

Check out Romans 3:23.

You mean . . . in the Bible?

You're quick.

Can't You just tell me what it says?

It's in the bookshelf . . . in the living room.

What?

Your Bible.

But—

That's why you want Me to tell you what it says—because you don't know where your Bible is.

This is scary.

No. It's reality. Wipe off the dust and turn to Romans 3:23.

Um—

It's right after Acts.

Yeah.

Which follows Luke.

Uh-huh.

New Testament.

Oh, yeah.

Got it?

Okay. Here it is: "For all have sinned and fall short of the glory of God." So?

So that's not just prostitutes. It's you too.

Hey! You can't compare me to a prostitute.

Why not? You're both sinners.

Yeah, but I don't sin like *they* do!

Hm. What do you think sin is?

You know . . . killing someone, having sex outside of marriage, robbing a store.

My child, sin is disobeying Me.

But disobeying You . . . well, that would include a lot more than just killing, sex, and robbing!

Right.

I mean, that would be a whole bunch of stuff.

Right.

Like lying. And saying bad words. And hating Mark, who's always giving me a hard time.

Right.

But if You define sin as anything that's in disobedience to You, then . . . how could *anyone* be good?

YES! You're getting it.

Getting what?

That's just it! NO ONE is good. Everyone has sinned. You were *born* with sin. And the sin you were born with is the same sin the prostitute and thief and murderer were born with.

But—I don't get it, God. That would put all of us in the same category and—

Exactly.

And I go to church.

Makes no difference.

And try to do good things.

Makes no difference.

And know about You.

Makes no difference at all, My child.

Well, if none of that makes any difference, why bother with it?

That's what I'd like to know.

Huh?

Why *do* you go to church?

Because I'm supposed to. I mean . . . because that's what Christians do. I mean . . . *sigh* . . . I don't know, God. I really don't know.

Tell me about your relationship with Grayson.

He's my best friend.

So have you always been best friends?

Seems that way. But, no. We first met on the playground during recess. I'd heard about him, because he was the new kid. I kept hearing he was this great athlete. So I kind of knew a lot about him even before we really became friends.

Go on.

Well, we were in the third grade. And one day during recess, he stole a base during our kickball game. I was on the opposing team and got mad at him because he got away with it. He was too fast for me.

Oh, so you didn't become friends as soon as you met each other?

No. Not right away. But a few weeks later, our P.E. teacher announced we were starting soccer season. He divided the class into two teams and made Grayson captain for one of the teams. When it came time to select players, Grayson asked me to be on his team. So I accepted. And it felt good. We weren't opponents anymore. We were playing together. We started hanging out. And talking. And we liked a lot of the same things. We just became best friends. And still are.

Okay, let's recap. You knew *about* Grayson before you actually knew him personally. And eventually, you accepted his invitation to join his team. And your friendship has grown consistently ever since.

Right.

Hello.

Huh?

Hello??? Are you hearing yourself? That's what Christianity is!

Stealing bases and playing soccer?

No. But stick with Me and you'll get it.

Please make this easy.

Like with Grayson, you know a lot *about* Me—but you don't really know Me personally.

Oh yes I—

Do you actually have a personal growing relationship with Me? Think about it before you answer. You knew a lot about Grayson, but you've already said you weren't his friend. You didn't really have a relationship with each other.

That's right. We didn't.

You shared a lot of the same interests, but you weren't playing on the same team.

Yeah. Even though we were playing the same game, we were actually playing against each other.

Until he invited you to be a part of *his* team.

And I accepted.

That's exactly what I'm doing. I'm inviting every single sinner in the world to become part of My team.

Ah. I think I'm getting it.

Will you accept My invitation?

But, God . . . I don't think I'm good enough to be on Your team. I mean, You've already said it—I'm a sinner.

And Grayson was really the better athlete. You admitted he was too fast for you. You could barely keep up.

Yeah, but he overlooked that. He wanted to be my friend anyway.

And I want to look past your sin. I want to erase it from your heart. It's a gift. My gift to You. All you have to do is accept it.

Wow. When You put it that way, I actually get it. I mean, I understand now. Christianity is really about admitting I'm a sinner and accepting Your forgiveness, huh?

Exactly.

And?

And what?

Well, there's gotta be more to it than that.

Yes. I'm not inviting you to make a spur-of-the-moment decision that will affect today only. I'm inviting you to become part of My great plan. I'm asking you to repent of your sin, accept My forgiveness, and allow Me to live inside of you, and in return, you follow My leading in every area of your life.

That sounds pretty incredible.

It is.

I mean it sounds . . . special.

It is.

I mean . . . it sounds like You're dreaming something up for me.

I am, My child. I'm dreaming BIG dreams for you.

I don't feel worthy, God.

You aren't. But I'm inviting you anyway.

I mean it sounds impossible. Too good to be true. What can I do to earn this kind of lifestyle?

You can't earn it.

But—

And you'll never be good enough to deserve it.

But—

It's a gift. I love you so incredibly much, I want to *give you* peace, purpose, forgiveness, joy, and eternal life.

Wow!

And I want to empower you with a strength beyond your imagination. I want to place My very Spirit inside of you.

That's what being a Christian is?

That's what being a Christian is.

It's a relationship.

Yes.

And it's forgiveness.

Yes.

And it's living for You.

Yes.

By *Your* strength . . . and in *Your* power.

Yes!

And living within Your dreams for my life!

Yes, My child! Yes!

I want that, Father! Will You forgive me right now?

Yes, I forgive you.

I admit it. I'm a sinner. And I see now that there's no difference between my little white lies, my cheating in school, and in murdering someone. All sin is sin.

I forgive you, My child.

I'm so sorry, God. I don't want to live in sin. I want to live in Your strength and power instead. Will You invade my life? Will You take over? Will You just go ahead and be in complete charge of my life?

Thank you. That's exactly where I want to be.

I'm not naive enough to think that I won't try to take charge of certain areas of my life again next week. Then what'll we do?

Then I'll bring it to your attention. That's *My* responsibility. That's what My Holy Spirit within you does. But you have a responsibility too.

What's that?

When I bring something to your attention, seek My forgiveness. Give it to Me.

And You'll forgive me?

Yes. And we'll keep walking together.

Sounds like a friendship. I mess up . . . we talk it out . . . we keep on keeping on.

It's called spiritual growth.

I love it!

And I love *you!*

So I'm a Christian now?

***Now* you're a Christian. You know Me personally.**

And You know what, God? Now I *want* to go to church! Now I *want* to live a life pleasing to You. Now I *wanna* be good!

Because you've allowed Me to change your heart.

But there's one other thing.

Yes?

Back to the dream thing.

The dream?

Yeah. Earlier, You said You were dreaming some big dreams for me.

That's right. I am.

I'm curious. Just how big *are* those dreams?

It's on the couch.

What is?

Your Bible.

But—

Pick it up and flip over to Ephesians 3:20. New Testament. Right before—

I got it! Right before Philippians. Hm, 3:20. Got it. "Now to him who is able to do immeasurably more than all we ask or imagine, according to his power that is at work within us."

Did you get it?

Immeasurably more?

You got it! Immeasurably more than you can even imagine, My child. That's what I dream for you.

Wow! Thanks so much, God, for helping me realize I really wasn't a Christian.

You are now.

Yeah. I am now.

On Divorce

I said: God, I'm hurting so bad I think I'll die!

God said: I know. My child.

Do You really, God? I'm falling apart.

I'm here. Let Me hold you.

I never knew anything could hurt this bad! God, do You have any idea what it's like to lose someone You love so much?

Yes, My child. I know exactly how you feel. I gave My Son and watched Him die so that others could live.

Hold me, God. Hold me!

Your dad is confused.

How could he?

And hurting.

But how could he just leave us?

***I'll* never leave you.**

I have friends who have gone through a divorce with their parents, but I never thought it would happen to me—to *my* family.

I know.

My heart is breaking, God.

Let Me help. My Spirit is a spirit of comfort. I've promised you the Comforter.

I need Your comfort.

I've promised you lots of things.

I need to be reminded.

Let Me comfort you and remind you of My love right now.

Yeah, I want that.

I'll use My Word to do that.

Okay.

I notice your Bible is open to Psalms.

Yeah. It's my favorite book.

Let's turn to Psalm 34:18.

"The LORD is close to the brokenhearted." Yes. That's what I need, God. My heart *is* broken. Thanks for being close to me.

And let's read Psalm 43:5.

Okay. "O my soul, why be so gloomy and discouraged? Trust in God! I shall again praise him for his wondrous help; he will make me smile again, *for he is my God!*" (TLB). Oh, Father, it feels like I'll never smile again—ever!

You will, My child. Trust Me. It will take time, but you *will* smile again. I promise.

Can I read You one of my favorites?

I'd love that.

It's 1 Peter 5:10. "And the God of all grace, who called you to his eternal glory in Christ, after you have suffered a little while, will himself restore you and make you strong, firm and steadfast."

It's true, My child. I will personally do that for you.

Thank You, Lord. It helps to read Your promises. But I'm hurting so badly!

I know. And I'm hurting with you. Every tear you shed flows down My face as well.

I feel betrayed. And angry. And guilty.

Guilty?

Yeah . . . that maybe there was something I could have done. Or maybe Dad's leaving was somehow my fault.

No. No. No. That's false guilt. There's not an ounce of truth in that.

But how do I know?

You'll have to trust Me.

Sometimes it's hard to trust what I can't see.

That's when you trust My words. Keep reading.

Okay. Here's another one of my favorites. "These [trials] have come so that your faith—of greater worth than gold, which perishes even though refined by fire—may be proved genuine and may result in praise, glory and honor when Jesus Christ is revealed. Though you have not seen him, you love him; and even though you do not see him now, you believe in him and are filled with an inexpressible and glorious joy" (1 Peter 1:7–8).

You're worth the world to me, My child. And, I promise, when you get through this trial, your faith will be much stronger.

I know that, God. I really believe that. But it still doesn't make it any easier.

I know.

The hurt runs incredibly deep. I mean . . . I lost my dad! He left us! He's gone! I feel incomplete. Lost.

But you're not. I'm here. And I will bring completion and wholeness and meaning and healing to you.

When will I stop hurting, God?

You won't.

Then how can I go on living?

This will always hurt you. Even when you're fifty years old, this will still hurt. But I can teach you not to focus on the hurt. I can bring

healing to your feelings of being left and deserted. And I can show you how to focus on all the good things I'm going to do in your life.

I need that, God. I need You to do that for me.

You're on the right track.

What do You mean?

You're doing exactly what I want you to do: You're telling Me everything, and you're being honest in how you feel. The more you share your hurt with Me, the more I heal and comfort and restore.

It feels like good things will never come my way again.

Nothing could be further from the truth.

I need a promise, God.

You've got it. Turn to Jeremiah 29:11.

Okay. Here it is: " 'For I know the plans I have for you,' declares the LORD, 'plans to prosper you and not to harm you, plans to give you hope and a future.' "

The sun *will* shine again, My child . . . as long as you keep focused on the Son.

I get it. I get it. Thank You, God. Thank You for knowing my hurt. For understanding. For not rushing me through the pain but being patient and just letting me talk and cry and hurt with You. I'm looking forward to the brighter moments You'll bring into my life.

Not just moments—celebrations! You can't imagine what I have in store for you!

Meanwhile . . . is it okay if I just sit here for a while?

Come here, My child. Crawl into My lap. Let Me wrap My arms of strength and comfort around your life.

Thank You, Lord. Thank You, Lord!

Close your eyes and bask in My love.

Thank You, God. Really. Thank You.

I'll never leave you. I'll never walk away. Rest, My child. Rest.

3

On Music and the Media

*W*hew! It's such a comfort to know that we don't have to wade through the tough times by ourselves. During those times when we're hurting so badly that we can't even express ourselves, God is there to strengthen us, hold us, and cry with us.

There's not a trial or a heartache we experience that He doesn't feel with us. He's that intimately involved in our lives.

During the days when we feel we can't put one foot in front of the other, He's there . . . offering assurance and hope.

"We are hard pressed on every side, but not crushed; perplexed, but not in despair; persecuted, but not abandoned; struck down, but not destroyed" (2 Corinthians 4:8–9).

Since God cares so much about *our* hurt, doesn't it make sense that we'd want to take every precaution in the world to keep from hurting *Him*? So often, we casually and callously allow things into our minds that break our Father's heart. As you read the next conversation, ask God if there's anything you need to shield yourself from that's causing a wedge between the two of you.

He said: When did you get that CD?

I said: Just today. Leisha loaned it to me after school.

I have a problem with it.

I like it.

Ever heard the phrase "garbage in, garbage out"?

Yeah.

It's true. Whatever you put into your mind will eventually show up in your lifestyle.

It doesn't affect me. I just like the music.

Hm. Mind if I listen *with* you?

Uh, that's okay, Jesus. This really isn't Your type of music.

Exactly. And if *I'm* not comfortable with it, why should you be?

Hey, I didn't say it was my fave album; I just *like* it.

Is it enhancing your relationship with Me?

You're kidding, right?

No. I was kidding when I made brussels sprouts. I'm not kidding about this. Does it enhance your relationship with Me?

Well . . . no. But that's not fair.

Why not?

Because . . . uh . . . popcorn doesn't enhance my relationship with You either. So is it wrong to eat popcorn?

No, there's nothing wrong with popcorn. You know that. But there *is* something wrong with the lyrics you're putting into your mind.

And . . . uh . . . those history specials my mom watches don't enhance my relationship with You either. So is it wrong to watch the History Channel?

You're missing the point. The History Channel—and popcorn—aren't putting stuff in your mind that goes directly against Me. The music you're listening to is filled with everything I oppose.

You mean the beat?

I mean the words.

But—

The message.

But—

Everything the artist is singing about.

But he's just singing about how angry he is. You got angry too, Jesus. Remember that part in the Bible when You got angry in the Temple and threw out the money changers?

Yes. That was righteous anger. I was angry about sin. I'd love for *you* to be angry about sin too! And since you brought up the Bible, where *is* yours?

Uh, I left it at church.

Then grab your mom's Bible. It's on top of her dresser.

Sigh. Okay. Now what?

Turn to Philippians 4:8 and read it to Me.

Here it is. "Finally, brothers, whatever is true, whatever is noble, whatever is right, whatever is pure, whatever is lovely, whatever is admirable—if anything is excellent or praiseworthy—think about such things."

Does the CD you're listening to fit into any of those categories?

Well . . .

Now grab that other Bible.

What other Bible?

Your mom has several versions in the bookshelf. Grab the Good News Bible.

Huh. I didn't even know we had this. Today's English Version? Hm.

Flip over to Proverbs 4:23.

Okay. "Be careful how you think; your life is shaped by your thoughts" (TEV).

Now pick up that New International Version you had a second ago. And read the same Scripture to Me.

Proverbs 4:23 again?

Right. This time from the NIV.

All right. "Above all else, guard your heart, for it is the wellspring of life." Huh.

Think about it.

I'm thinking.

Are you getting it?

No.

Your mind and your heart are connected.

They are?

Whatever you listen to obviously goes directly into your head.

Yeah.

But it doesn't just stay there.

So where's it go?

It goes to your heart as well.

Ouch.

It's impossible for a human to say, "It doesn't affect me." I created humans. I know better. It *has* to affect you, because that's the way

you're wired. Whatever goes into your head eventually seeps into your heart. And your lifestyle is an overflow of everything inside your heart. Your thoughts and your affections control how you act, react, and live.

Wow. That sounds pretty complicated.

It is. But it doesn't have to be.

I just wanted to borrow this CD because *everyone's* listening to it and talking about it. I didn't mean to do something harmful.

I know you didn't. And that's why it's important that we talk . . . about *everything*.

What do You mean?

Your responsibility as a Christian is to follow Me. But it's My responsibility as your Savior to lead you in the way I want you to go.

Yeah.

Sometimes you'll take a wrong turn.

Like today?

Right. And when you do, I'll always let you know. I'll often speak through your heart or through your mind.

Like You're doing right now?

Exactly. But if your heart and mind become cluttered with things of the world, it'll become harder and harder for you to hear My voice.

Oh! I get it!

As long as you have a pure and tender heart, I can continue working in your life. You'll hear My voice. I'll make My will known to you.

But when I allow a bunch of garbage inside me, I won't hear Your voice.

Right.

Lord, I *want* a pure heart!

I know you do, My child.

And I *wanna* know Your voice.

And I'm anxious to share it with you.

But does that mean I can't ever listen to stuff that's not Christian?
No. But it *does* mean you need to depend on My Holy Spirit to direct you. And to do that, you need to be in constant communication with Me.
So not all secular stuff is bad?
The key, My child, is learning discernment. And that's what My Spirit excels in.
I don't get it.
Instead of simply saying, "I'll never listen to anything that doesn't praise God," I'd rather teach you how to make wise choices.
I'm listening.
If you determine never to let anything nonreligious into your life, you'll have to exclude opera, ballet, and classical and jazz music. And you'll need to stay away from poetry and nursery rhymes and the nightly news.
Oh, yeah!
Grab your mom's Bible again, and read John 15:19.
"As it is, you do not belong to the world, but I have chosen you out of the world."
And check out Romans 12:2.
Okay. "Do not conform any longer to the pattern of this world, but be transformed by the renewing of your mind. Then you will be able to test and approve what God's will is—his good, pleasing and perfect will." Wow.
My child, you can't help but live in the world. This is where I've placed you. But take great caution not to become part of the world around you.
I think I'm getting it, but could You keep going? I'm almost there.
There's nothing wrong with reading the newspaper. You live in this world—it makes sense to know what's going on in the world in which you live.
Yeah.

And there are some beautiful sonnets and fun nursery rhymes and other creative works that don't mention My name but aren't evil.

That's true.

Just because I'm not talked about in every song, novel, or theatrical experience doesn't mean it's bad. I'm the Creator of all that's good.

Oh, yeah!

I invented rhyme and music and color and humor and mystery and romance and laughter and love.

Yeah!

It's only when those things are used in evil ways that they become sin.

Like when the music or art or theater or whatever showcases stuff that goes against Your character, then it's wrong.

Absolutely.

I get it. I'm really getting it, Jesus. You're not a kill-joy.

No.

You're not out to take away my love of music, my rhythm, or my dramatic flair. You're out to protect my mind and my heart. You really love me, don't You, Jesus?

Beyond your wildest imagination!

And You wanna protect my heart and my head so that I'll always hear Your voice and follow You!

Right.

Jesus, let's go to the family room.

Why?

Cuz I'm feeling creative, and I'd love to use my energy to write a song or a poem or something that glorifies You.

I'd like nothing better. But there's something I want you to do first.

What's that?

Let's take that CD out of your stereo.

Gotcha. I'm sorry, Lord. I really am. I don't know what I was thinking. Will You forgive me?

You're forgiven.

Can we just forget about this?

It's already forgotten.

And will You help me to make wise media choices? I really want to keep a pure heart.

There's nothing I'd like better.

4

On God's Love

God said: I love you.

I said: Yeah, I know.

Do you *really* know?

Sure. God is love. Love is God. God is love.

But do you *believe*?

You're kidding, right? I've had John 3:16 memorized since I was eight.

But do you really *believe* it? In other words, are you living your life by it?

Living my life by it?

Meaning . . . if you really *know* it and *believe* it, how are you allowing it to affect the way you live?

Well . . . I don't know that it actually *affects* me. . . .

It *could.* In fact, your entire life can be better when you *really* buy into the fact that I LOVE YOU.

I *think* I've bought into it, Lord.

Give me an example.

Okay. Uh . . . yesterday, I really wanted to watch reruns of my favorite TV show when I got home from school, but my little sister was watching *Road Runner.* Instead of trying to talk her into switching channels, I just sat down and watched it with her. Felt kind of good to do the right thing instead of demanding my own way. Later, when I went to bed, I knew You were smiling at me.

You're right. I was. I loved you so much right then, I felt like I was going to burst.

And I could feel it!

But you know what?

What?

I felt the very same love for you this morning when you snubbed Juli between first and second period.

Did You hear what she was saying about me? It was so unfair! So untrue! Who does she think she is? Lord, I know I should have been kind, but I just felt so much anger. I'm sorry.

I know. But even then—when you *should* have been forgiving, I was bursting with love for you.

But, God, how *could* You? I . . .

And last Thursday. Remember that pop quiz in history?

I was hoping You hadn't noticed.

I'm God. I notice *everything.* That's part of the job.

Well, I just wasn't prepared. I mean, after all . . . I went to youth group on Wednesday night. I never got a chance to study. So when Mrs. Woodard tossed a quiz at us at the last minute . . . well, I didn't have a choice. I *had* to cheat.

You always have a choice.

I know it was wrong. And I feel gross about it. But it's not like I make a practice of doing that. I *never* cheat.

Still—in that moment—even when you were clearly doing something that you knew was wrong . . . I was bursting with love for you.

I feel so guilty.

And last Saturday night?

Can we just skip over this one?

When you came in at 12:30 A.M.—thirty minutes past your curfew . . .

Well, God, it's not like I actually lied.

And Sunday morning at the breakfast table when your dad said, "What time did you come in last night, Kelli?" And you said—

All I said was, "Are you kidding, Dad? I know my curfew is midnight. Think I'd even *consider* breaking it?"

Which was deceptive.

But true. Cuz I do know when my curfew is.

But false because you not only *considered* breaking it—you *broke* it. And deceptive because you actually deceived your dad into thinking you came in on time when you really didn't.

Well . . . at least I didn't *lie.*

What IS a lie?

That's easy. It's saying something happened when it didn't.

Hm. And you led your dad into believing you were in at midnight. Isn't that—

Saying something happened when it didn't? No. Yes. I mean, uh . . . I don't know. Look, God, isn't it about time for my devotions or something? This is getting pretty heavy. I really ought to go now. You know—read my Bible or something.

Well, you're *half* right. *Devotions* is simply a term for spending time with Me. Part of that time should be spent reading My Word— the Bible—and the other part should be spent talking with Me.

And I have. It's been great, God. Gotta go.

AND listening to what I have to say.

Go on.

Even then . . . early Sunday morning . . . when you were sneaking in past your curfew and lying about it a few hours later, I was bursting with love for you.

God, stop. Please. I can't handle this. I . . . . I'm so ashamed.

And I love you.

I'm so far from what I should be.

And I love you.

So incomplete from whom You've called me to be.

And I love you.

I fail so much.

And I love you.

I do stuff I know I shouldn't.

And I love you.

Please forgive me, Father. I am so sorry.

You're forgiven. And on top of that . . . why don't we just wipe the slate clean?

You mean? . . .

Let's live as though these things never even happened.

But . . .

As of now, I choose to forget them.

But, God. How can You do that?

I love you.

I know, but . . . how can You love me when I'm a jerk?

My child, I'm hurt when you disobey Me. And, like a loving parent, I correct you and call you to obedience. But I *never* stop loving you.

You mean even when I slip and talk bad about Jason . . .

My Holy Spirit pricks your conscience, and I remind you that's wrong. You need to ask My forgiveness. But I still love you.

Well, what about the times I snap back to Mom and Dad?

I rebuke you and correct you and call you to submit to their authority. But My love for you is the same as if you'd *never* talked back.

And when others don't like me? When I don't make the volleyball team? What about when I run for class office and get only twenty-eight votes?

Even then. My love remains the same. I'm bursting with love for you.

But when I've gained six pounds? And when I'm not careful about what I eat? And when I have zits on my nose? And . . .

And even then, I *love* you—regardless of what you look like or act like. Learn to live and grow in My love. Let it affect every single area of your life.

I think I'm beginning to understand.

When you really learn to accept My unconditional love for you, you can't help but be changed.

I . . . I'm *getting* it. *You* love *me* so much, I want to love You back. I really do, God. It's clear now. Oh, Father! I want to please You. I want to obey You. I want to love You with my lifestyle. I want others to see You in my actions and reactions.

Yes!

I gotta go, Lord.

Oh?

Yeah. I need to talk to Mrs. Woodard about last week's quiz.

I'm proud of you.

And then I'm gonna call Dad at the office.

5

On Hypocrisy

*I*t's hard to swallow: God loves us NMW—no matter what! We've broken His heart, we've disobeyed Him, and we've ignored Him, yet He continues to love us and completely forgive us. When we finally come to the realization that there's nothing we can do to make Him love us any more, and nothing we can do to make Him love us any less . . . we want to respond in obedience to Him.

"Jesus replied, 'If anyone loves me, he will obey my teaching. My Father will love him, and we will come to him and make our home with him. He who does not love me will not obey my teaching'" (John 14:23–24).

So what's the proof of our love for God? You choose. Mark the right answer:

a. ____ perfect church attendance
b. ____ saying the right words at the right time
c. ____ being as nice as we possibly can
d. ____ obeying God's commands

And if we're committed to obeying God, it will affect every area of our lives—our actions and reactions, the jokes we tell, the stuff we read, what we watch and listen to . . . even what we wear. After all, why bother wearing a gold cross if the life behind it doesn't match the symbol? Hm. Same goes for wearing the WWJD bracelet or a T-shirt embossed with Christian symbols or carrying your Bible to school. As you read the next conversation, ask God if your "walk" matches your "talk."

God said: Nice touch.

I said: Thanks. But . . . what are we talking about?

That WWJD bracelet you're wearing.

Oh. Yeah, I've got five.

I know. You can match 'em with just about anything in your closet, can't you?

Yeah. Cool, huh?

You've got a pretty good collection.

Yep.

Too bad it's not more.

Well, I'll get a few more—eventually. After all, they *do* cost.

No, I'm not talking about adding more bracelets to your collection. But, you're right—there *is* a cost involved.

Uh-oh. I've got a feeling we're not on the same page, are we, God?

Nope.

Look, I'm kind of in a hurry, Lord. So if You have something to say, could You just say it?

I already have.

Guess I didn't catch it.

Let's go through it again, okay? Check out 1 John 2:4-5.

Uh. All right. Gimme a sec.

It's under your bed.

What?

Your Bible.

How'd You know that's what I was look—

I'm God, remember? I know everything.

Oh, yeah. Okay. Here we go: "Someone may say, 'I am a Christian; I am on my way to heaven; I belong to Christ.' But if he doesn't do what Christ tells him to, he is a liar. But those who do what Christ tells them to will learn to love God more and more. That is the way to know whether or not you are a Christian" (TLB).

So . . . lay it on me, God. What are You saying?

I'm saying it sure would be nice if that WWJD bracelet you're wearing were more than a fashion statement. But if it were . . . it would cost.

Hey, wait a sec! I'm not just wearing this as a fad! I know what it stands for. I believe in it.

Believing in a phrase and living the lifestyle are two different things.

I'm listening.

Well, to *really* live out the WWJD lifestyle may cost you some dates.

Guys?

And maybe some friends.

The girls?

And maybe your time.

My TV shows?

**WWJD means asking yourself, "What would Jesus do" before any-
thing and everything you do.**

Well, yeah . . . *technically.*

Excuse Me?

I mean, yeah . . . we all know that's what the *letters* stand for.

But . . .

But to take it *seriously.* I mean to actually *ask ourselves* that question
. . . well, that would change everything—or at least *a lot!*

Check out 1 John 2:6.

Okay. Got it right here. "Anyone who says he is a Christian should live
as Christ did" (TLB).

Hm.

**So what's it gonna be? A fashion statement or a lifestyle backed
with commitment?**

But God, I'm not sure You really understand. If I truly asked what
would You do . . . well, You probably wouldn't go to the movie I'm
gonna see this Friday with Brian.

Not that particular one; no.

And You probably wouldn't want me hanging out with Kari as much.
**She shoplifts. And since you're not doing anything to confront her
or trying to introduce her to Me, she's pulling you down. Yeah, I'd
like you to quit spending so much time with her.**

God, if I start asking myself that question . . .

If you *don't,* and you continue to wear that bracelet, you're a phony.

That's a bit harsh, don't You think?

**Read My words again. The ones in 1 John 2:4. Read the last part
of that verse.**

"But if he doesn't do what Christ tells him to, he is a liar" (TLB).

Ouch.

Yes . . . *ouch.* I died for those words.

I know.

I also died to give you the power you need to put those words into practice.

I'm not that strong, God.

I know. I made you, remember? I realize you're weak. I know your temptations. But I can equip you with everything you need to become all I call you to be.

You know what this means, don't You? There may be a few Friday nights I'm home alone.

No, not alone. I've promised never to leave you. I would *love* to spend Friday night with you.

Is this for real?

So real I shed My blood.

But . . . Friday night . . . alone with God?

Oh, My child, the things I want to do in your life! The dreams I want to give you! The vision I want to create with you. I have so much in store for you, your mind couldn't comprehend it all if I told you everything right now.

Wow. For *me?* That's kind of exciting!

For you. You're that special. I dream big dreams for you.

I'm pretty good at dreaming too, God.

Yes, you are. But My dreams are even bigger than your imagination! Check out Ephesians 3:20.

Okay, here it is: "Now glory be to God who by his mighty power at work within us is able to do far more than we would ever dare to ask or even dream of—infinitely beyond our highest prayers, desires, thoughts, or hopes" (TLB).

And what about Jeremiah 29:11?

Old Testament. Got it. "For I know the plans I have for you, says the

Lord. They are plans for good and not for evil, to give you a future and a hope" (TLB).

Wow.

My child, I love you way too much to let you slide. It hurts Me to watch you settle for WWJD being a mere piece of fabric wrapped around your wrist when it's meant to be so much more.

I'm sorry, Lord. I never really thought about it.

You see, I died for you, and went through more torture than you can even fathom . . . just so you could *love* WWJD instead of simply wear it.

This is a lot to swallow.

And I did it because I love you.

But Lord, I don't deserve a love that great.

And you know what? If you had been the only person in the entire world, I still would have gone through the crucifixion just for *you!*

Jesus, will You forgive me? I'm so sorry. I never meant to take Your death for granted. I don't want to be a phony. I want to be genuine and full of You. I want people to see a difference in my life. I'm sorry I've taken You for granted. Jesus, fill me. Saturate me. Control me. Let me be putty in Your hands. Remake me in Your image.

Yes!

I need to hurry to my piano lesson right now, Lord. And as soon as that's over, I have an important appointment.

Oh?

With my Bible and my heavenly Father. We need to talk about my friends, my time, and my entertainment.

Guess what?

What?

That's exactly what Jesus would do!

6

On Spending Time with God

It's easy to sit in front of a computer and become so involved in a chat room that we lose all awareness of time. Before we know it, an hour has flown by. And we can spend at least that much time with a phone connected to our ear sharing the latest with our best friend. I know many teens who rush to the computer as soon as they get home from school to see if they have e-mail waiting for them.

It's natural to spend time with those we care about. We want to know what happened in their day, what's going on with their lives and if anything new has developed.

That's communication. That's friendship. But the greatest Friend you'll ever have *also* wants to communicate with you. He waits patiently and yearns for you to talk with Him about everything that concerns you.

As you absorb the next conversation, evaluate your quiet time with God. Do you have one? Is it in balance with the rest of your activities? Do you need to make some changes?

God said: I miss talking with you.
I said: What? I just prayed on Sunday.
How often do you talk with Katie?
I dunno.
Think about it.
Well, okay. Let's see . . . we usually hang together before school, then we have English and math together. And—oh yeah—we've got study hall together in the afternoon. And lunch. I forgot about lunch. We eat lunch together every day.
So how often do you talk with Katie?
I guess all the time. We call each other a few times during the week to check on homework stuff. Yeah, I'd say pretty much all the time. But she *is* my best friend!
How often do you talk with Me?
I don't know.
Think about it.
Sigh. Well . . . on Sundays at church—and at youth group. You know.
I'd *love* to talk with you more.

But God, I already give You chitchat time.

I want more than chitchat. I'd like for you to tell Me everything.

Everything?

Why not? I already know what you're thinking anyway.

Yeah. And that's just it! If You know everything, what's the big deal about me having to talk with You?

***Having* to talk? Hm. I was hoping it would be more of an enjoyment instead of an obligation.**

Ah, You know what I mean.

You're right, I do. And that's exactly what hurts Me. Most of the time when you speak with Me, it's because you feel you're supposed to, or it's because your back is against the wall and you need help—fast.

I didn't know You felt that way.

My child, I paid the highest price I could pay for you. I long to be with you and to hear you voice your thoughts, your joys, your tears, your loneliness, your victories.

Well, okay. If it really means that much to You. But I still don't get this prayer thing. If You already know what I'm going to say before I even say it, what's the point in telling You?

It's the process.

Huh?

Remember last week when Katie took first place in the track meet?

Sure! I remember. Boy, was she excited!

Yes. And *you* were too.

Well, yeah. I *am* her best friend. You know.

But you actually heard about it *before* Katie told you.

Oh, yeah! Jason told me before I even saw Katie.

But when Katie rushed to you, waving her ribbon, you were just as happy and proud for her as if you were hearing the news for the first time.

Yeah.

That's friendship. That's relationship. That's love. Would you have wanted her to keep the news from you since you already knew?

No way! I love it when Katie gets excited. Her face lights up with that crooked grin, and her eyes glow like sparklers.

I feel the same way.

Hm.

I not only *love* for you to tell Me everything—I can't wait to hear it!

I think I'm starting to understand.

I'm not finished with Katie yet.

Oh?

Yeah. Let's keep talking about your friendship for just a bit longer.

Okay.

The more you two share (secrets, giggles, notes), and the more you two do (trips together, youth group parties, football games), the closer you become.

So it's doing stuff that makes us such great friends, right?

Partly right. But I really want you to think about this, okay?

Okay.

It's also the p-r-o-c-e-s-s.

I'm thinking.

The *time* invested in sharing and doing.

Yeah. I get it. We're sort of investing ourselves in each other's lives.

Exactly. And your friendship is growing because of it.

Yeah! Cool.

Do you hear what I'm saying?

Keep talking. I'm listening, God. I really am. I *want* to get this.

Your relationship with Me is pretty static right now.

Static?

Yeah. Dull. Boring.

I didn't think You noticed stuff like that.

I'm God, remember?

Oh, yeah.

But it doesn't have to be static. Don't forget, I *died* so we could have a relationship—an exciting, fun relationship, not a boring one.

Well, what can I do?

Spend time with Me. Talk to Me. When you cry, let Me wipe your tears. When you ace a history exam, share your good news with Me. When Lisa snubs you in the hallway, tell Me how bad it hurts. I want our relationship to grow.

Wow. Lord, I've never even thought of all that. I mean, why would You be so interested in my everyday, ordinary life?

Because I love you. Oh, how I love you!

Jesus, I'm sorry. I've pretty much left You on the shelf. I mean, yeah, I go to church, and I even read my Bible at times, and people know I'm a Christian. But You want me to grow in You too, and I haven't been—I've been static, just like You said. Will You forgive me?

I forgive you.

Jesus, I *want* to have a best-friend, Lord-of-lords relationship with You. I want You to *own* me and consume me.

Yes! That's what I want too. And you know what?

What?

I love the way you're praying right now.

Praying? I'm not praying. We're just talking.

Yeah. And that's exactly what prayer is.

I get it.

Open, honest, consistent communication.

I can't wait till tomorrow morning.

Why's that?

I'm going to get up early and pray.

You don't have to wait till tomorrow morning. Talk to Me when you get up at 1:30 A.M. to go to the bathroom.

Really?

Sure! And at 3:00 A.M. when you're tossing in bed and scrunching your pillow.

Hey! How'd You know I always—oh, yeah, You're God.

Right.

Well, in that case, how about hanging out right now? I've got some stuff I need to talk with You about.

Great. This is the moment I've been waiting for.

7

On Boyfriends

I said: *Sigh*. The start of another school year. And once again . . . I'm alone.

God said: Hello.

Well, okay—not *totally* alone. I have lunch with Heather and history with Natasha.

Hello?

Oh, yeah. And You're here, but that doesn't really count.

Excuse Me?

Well, You know. You're *God*. You're everywhere. That's Your job—to always hang around.

Yes, I *am* God. And true, I am omnipresent. But the reason I'm always with you is because I *choose* to be with you.

Hm. I never thought of it that way.

And I'm going to school with you, because I really, really want to.

41

Let's start this year *together*.
I appreciate that, God. I truly do.
But . . .
But—well, You know. Sometimes it helps to have *people*. I'm still gonna feel all alone.
But you've already mentioned Heather and Natasha.
Well, yeah.
They're people.
Yeah.
And they're good friends of yours.
I know, but still . . .
That's not enough?
Right. Because, well, You know. They're girls.
Ah.
Father, it seems like everyone has a boyfriend except me. I really want a guy this year!
Why is that so important to you?
Because I want to be like everyone else. I mean—wait a sec. I didn't mean . . .
I think you did, My child.
Well, all right. But I didn't mean to sound so shallow. Like the only reason I want a boyfriend is just to be like everybody else at school.
You know what? I absolutely adore honesty. And you're being honest with Me. Yes, there's a large part of you that *does* want a boyfriend for all the wrong reasons. But your reasons aren't totally out in left field.
Whaddya mean?
Everyone wants to feel included—a part of something. That's not necessarily bad. It's totally okay to yearn for acceptance. In fact, I created you that way—to belong and to be connected to other people.
Yeah! So are we gonna get me a guy?
BUT—to have a boyfriend simply to have a boyfriend is using someone for your own personal satisfaction.

Well . . .

Relationships are meant to be cherished. As you know, I place high value on people. I watched my Son die for them, remember?

I remember. And I'm grateful. I don't ever want to take His death for granted. But aren't we getting a little off the subject here? All I'm asking for is a boyfriend.

No. You're really asking for a lot more. You want to fit in—to be like everyone else—which again, isn't necessarily wrong. But how you go about it can *make* it wrong. And you're asking for a boyfriend as if he's a "thing," like the latest fad bracelet or the newest pair of athletic shoes. You're expecting that having a boyfriend will make you feel complete.

Finally! Now we're on the same track.

I don't think so, My child.

But You just said a boyfriend will make me complete!

No. I said that's what you're *thinking*.

Yeah! So let's get on with it. I really don't care what color his hair is . . .

No, My child. You're not listening.

Sure I am. We're talking about my guy here.

No. We're talking about *you*.

God, we are *sooo* not on the same page. I totally don't get where You're headed.

I'm headed into you. I am so in love with you, you'll never fully be able to comprehend it.

Yeah, but what's that got to do with me getting a boyfriend?

Everything. You see, My child, another person will never make you complete. No human being in the whole world can ever make you whole.

Well, I don't know about that. Eric Padesco comes pretty close!

Your fulfillment—your wholeness—can only be found in a solid, intimate, growing relationship with your Creator.

Wait a sec. Are You talking about *You*?

Yes, I am. I want to be your fulfillment. I am the only One Who can truly satisfy you.

But I'd be pretty satisfied with a guy too, God.

Another person can *enhance* your fulfillment, but he can't *be* your fulfillment.

I'm not totally getting it yet, but I'm interested. Go on.

I yearn (repeat: I y-e-a-r-n) to be your everything. I want to be your security, your confidence, your happiness, your wholeness, your purpose, your fulfillment, your all.

Wow.

Because when your security and your self-image and your wholeness are truly based on *Me*, it won't matter who's in your life or who's not in your life. Your purpose and self-esteem won't fluctuate because they'll be grounded in Me.

Keep going.

Okay. Pick up your Bible.

Uh . . .

It's underneath your math book.

Hey, how'd You know I was gonna ask . . .

Because I'm God, remember? I know everything.

Oh, yeah.

Flip over to James 1:17.

Philemon. Hebrews . . . James. Okay, I've got it.

Will you read it aloud?

Sure. "Every good and perfect gift is from above, coming down from the Father of the heavenly lights"—Cool! You're gonna give me a gift. You're giving me a boyfriend! Thank You! THANK You! THANK YOU!

Whoa, girl. You haven't even come to the portion of Scripture I want to talk with you about.

You're kidding!?!

I'm really not. Keep reading, please.

Sigh. All right. Let's see, uh, "Father of the heavenly lights, who does not change like shifting shadows."

Does not change.

So . . .

So when you allow *Me* to complete you, you're placing yourself in an unshakable Security.

Does. Not. Change.

Does not change. I'm immovable. I don't even shift *slightly* like a shadow does.

You're always there. You do not move.

I'm always here. I never move.

So I can be totally secure without a guy!

***If* your security is placed in Me.**

And I really don't have to worry about what others are thinking. . . .

. . . If you'll allow *Me* to fulfill you.

I'm getting it, Father. Wow!

Yes!

That's what I want, God. That's truly what I want!

Will you trust Me to bring the right relationships into your life at just the right time?

I want to. But to be honest, I still kinda want to control this one part of my life.

I adore your honesty!

So can I keep this part of my life?

Not if you want *Me* to be your total fulfillment.

I do, God. I really, really do.

My child, trust that I want your fulfillment—even more than you do!

Yeah.

Repeat after Me: My loving, heavenly Father . . .

My loving, heavenly Father . . .

. . . wants my fulfillment . . .

. . . wants my fulfillment . . .

. . . even more than I do!

. . . even more than I do!

Are you getting it?

I am, Father. There may be times when I wish I had what someone else has, but I'll remember You truly *are* all I need.

My timing is perfect. When I want a guy in your life, I'll make it happen. But please trust *Me* with it. As much as you want to make it happen yourself, please trust Me.

I will.

Oh, and one more thing. Try memorizing Habakkuk 2:3.

Ha-whata-kuk?

Old Testament. Between Nahum and Zephaniah.

Sheesh!! Was everyone just really hard up for names back then or what?

We did have some doozies, didn't we? Found it yet?

I've got it. Habakkuk 2:3. Okay if I read this one outta *The Living Bible?*

Sure.

"But these things I plan won't happen right away. Slowly, steadily, surely, the time approaches when the vision will be fulfilled. If it seems slow, do not despair, for these things will surely come to pass. Just be patient! They will not be overdue a single day!" (TLB).

I love that.

I'm never early, My child. And I'm never late.

It's gonna be a good school year, Father.

How do you know?

Because I'm trusting You. And because we'll go through it together.

Right! Now let's get started on your history assignment.

Let's? As in You and me?

We're in this thing together, remember?

Yeah . . . but are You any good at history?

Are you kidding? I created it.

When "everyone else" is in a relationship, it's easy to feel left out. That's normal. God created us as relational beings. We want to belong. We want to give. We need to be needed.

But before God can develop these areas in us—helping us to connect with another person—He first wants to make sure our connection with Him is able to survive without other relationships. Yeah, it's easy to *read* about giving God control of our dating life, our future relationships, and even our someday-to-be-met mate. It's another thing to actually *do* it.

Hey, if you haven't truly placed God in control of your past, present, and future relationships, *right now* is the perfect time to do it. Go ahead. No one's watching. Just say a quiet little prayer right now and tell Him He's in charge.

8

On Language

Yeah, I know. Unless you're marooned on an uninhabited island, alone and fighting for survival, you can't help but be surrounded by stuff with which God isn't pleased. Just flipping through the channels searching for something decent, you'll have to wade through a plethora of sights and sounds that are anything but Christlike.

Just walking through the mall, you'll hear language and notice all the clothes people *aren't* wearing. How in the world can you shield yourself from all the filth? Is it possible to live IN the world yet not be part OF the world?

Not in your own strength. But by tapping into a supernatural power—God's Holy Spirit—you *can* live a holy life. It all happens in your mind. Check out what the Bible says in Romans 12:2: "Do not conform any longer to the pattern of this world, but be transformed by the renewing of your mind. Then you will be able to test and approve what God's will is—his good, pleasing and perfect will."

As you enter into the next conversation with God, ask Him to show you anything in your life that's displeasing to Him. When He does, be ready to place that area in His control.

God said: It needs to bother you.

I said: What?

The language.

What language?

Case in point. You haven't even noticed.

I'm not tracking with You. Notice what?

My name's being taken in vain.

Oh, that. Well, God, to be honest with You . . . I've kind of gotten used to it.

Used to it?

Well, yeah. My school hallways are filled with conversations echoing Your name. Not only that, but it's pretty much a smorgasbord of four-letter options too.

And that doesn't affect you?

Nah. Like I said, I'm used to it.

That's the problem.

Whaddya mean?

I don't *want* you to get *used* to it.

But I hear that stuff all the time. TV's full of it. Every sitcom I watch tosses Your name around. Can we get personal? Is it really that big of a deal?

Apparently you don't realize the severity of this.

Guess not.

Every single time someone says, "Oh, my God!" they're breaking one of My Ten Commandments: "Thou shalt not take the name of the Lord Thy God in vain."

Yeah, but—

Doing something I've specifically spoken against is a big deal.

Well—

I call it sin.

But not *real* sin. Right?

Excuse Me?

I always thought sin was like . . . You know . . . murdering someone or stealing something.

Sin is anything that goes against what I've commanded.

But Father, practically *everyone* says stuff like, "Oh, God."

Not *everyone* is going to heaven.

Well, *I* don't say it. Well, okay, maybe once . . . twice max.

But you've become comfortable with hearing it. That's just as bad.

Well, I—

My child, I don't want you to get comfortable living in this world and hearing what goes on around you. You see, this world really isn't your home. Think of it as sort of a holding tank. Your *real* home is in heaven with Me. And the splendor of it is beyond your capability of human understanding.

I know, God. And I'm looking forward to that.

But you'll never get to spend eternity with Me if you constantly choose sin over Me. If you love Me, you will turn from your sin. And using My name in such a flippant manner is certainly sin.

Wow. I didn't realize.

You can't help living in this world I've placed you in. But you *can* choose not to be a part of it.

How do I do that?

By refusing to get comfortable.

Go on.

I realize there are things you can't help but hear, but that doesn't mean you should become accustomed to hearing them. I want your stomach to bunch up in knots when you hear My name used in the wrong way. I want you to feel uncomfortable when people around you share coarse jokes and brag about their sexual escapades. I want you to turn around and walk away when you hear or see sin.

That will take a conscious effort, Father.

I know.

But, do You think if I could get into the habit of doing it, it would become almost as natural as breathing?

You're catching on.

It will be hard.

You won't be alone.

People will probably laugh at me when I refuse to listen to their sug- gestive conversations.

A few will respect you.

It would be easier if I had an example.

Ahem.

You know someone else who has already taken a stand?

Study My Son's life.

Oh, yeah!

And read Hebrews chapter 11. It's FULL of people who took a stand.

Yeah, but some of *them* were *killed* for their beliefs.

That's what Christianity's all about.

Dying???

That's right.

Dying???

Yes. My true disciples are the ones who have died for living their own lives. They've given up control. They've become putty in My hands, and they're letting Me reshape and remold them in My image. Read what I say about it in Galatians 2:20.

Okay. I've got it: "I have been crucified with Christ; and I myself no longer live, but Christ lives in me" (TLB).

And I guess that's what You want for me?

I want you to spend eternity with Me in heaven, and I need you to die to your own selfish habits, your coarse language, your plans for the future, your selfishness—even your rights.

But God—

And guess what?

What?

When you do . . . you'll start to become very uncomfortable with the world around you.

9

On Hell

*I*t's easy to become so comfortable in the world in which we live that another dimension seems almost unbelievable. But throughout the Bible, God goes to great lengths to show us beyond doubt that there *is* life after death. He wastes no words in making sure we realize that after death, we'll face judgment. And after judgment, we'll spend eternity in either heaven or hell.

Since we don't hear many pastors preaching on damnation and eternal hell, it's easy to forget that hell actually exists. It seems more like a spicy word used to punctuate every other paragraph on TV sitcoms and dramas. But hell isn't simply a curse word; it's a place.

One way to take hell seriously is to fear it. As you dive into this next conversation, ask God to help you develop a godly fear of hell.

I said: There's something I'd like to talk to You about, God.

God said: Great! I love it when you come to Me. What's on your mind?

Well . . . hell.

Hell?

Yeah. I've heard all my life that people who don't know You are going to hell.

That's right.

But is hell really that bad?

What do *you* think?

Well, I'll just tell You what I've heard, okay?

Okay.

I've heard some people say hell will be whatever makes you the most miserable.

Hm. So, if doing homework really ticks you off, hell will be eternal homework?

Yeah, I guess.

That would be punishment all right, but do you really think someone like, oh, I don't know, let's say Hitler—who was responsible for *millions* of deaths and human torture—will be sitting around for eternity writing book reports?

When You put it that way, it sounds kinda lame.

Yeah, and hell is not lame. It's beyond your imagination. It's a place you wanna make sure you stay away from. Of course, you realize you can't do that in your own strength, right?

Yeah, I've got that part. I know I can't save myself from hell. That's something only You can do.

Right. And that's where total surrender comes in.

I'm with You. But I'm still not sure I've got the whole picture.

What else have you heard?

That someday You'll take all the Christians to heaven and everyone else will be left here on earth, and that will be hell because there will be no love or kindness.

That *will* be bad. But hell is more than simply a void of love and kindness.

So . . . just how bad *is* it? And *what* is it?

Since you've heard what others have to say about it, why not take a peek at *My* words concerning hell.

Yeah, I'd like that. I don't have a Bible with one of those fancy concordances, so I really don't even know where to look.

That's okay. I'll guide you.

Thanks.

I've given a pretty graphic description of hell. In fact, *every* time it's mentioned in the Bible, you'll notice that it's defined as a place of great torment and agony. I describe it as an actual *place* . . . a lake of fire.

Yuck.

Way more than yuck. Grab your Bible, okay? Tell Me what you think of *this* picture of hell found in Luke 16:19-31.

Okay. Here it is:

> "There was a certain rich man," Jesus said, "who was splen-
> didly clothed and lived each day in mirth and luxury. One day
> Lazarus, a diseased beggar, was laid at his door. As he lay

there longing for scraps from the rich man's table, the dogs
would come and lick his open sores. Finally the beggar died
and was carried by the angels to be with Abraham in the place
of the righteous dead [heaven]. The rich man also died and
was buried, and his soul went into hell. There, in torment, he
saw Lazarus in the far distance with Abraham.

" 'Father Abraham,' he shouted, 'have some pity! Send
Lazarus over here if only to dip the tip of his finger in water
and cool my tongue, for I am in anguish in these flames.'

"But Abraham said to him, 'Son, remember that during
your lifetime you had everything you wanted, and Lazarus had
nothing. So now he is here being comforted and you are in
anguish. And besides, there is a great chasm [distance] sepa-
rating us, and anyone wanting to come to you from here is
stopped at its edge; and no one over there can cross to us.'

"Then the rich man said, 'O Father Abraham, then please
send him to my father's home—for I have five brothers—to
warn them about this place of torment lest they come here
when they die.'

"But Abraham said, 'The Scriptures have warned them again
and again. Your brothers can read them any time they want to.'

"The rich man replied, 'No, Father Abraham, they won't
bother to read them. But if someone is sent to them from the
dead, then they will turn from their sins.'

"But Abraham said, 'If your brothers won't listen to Moses
and the prophets, they won't listen even though someone
rises from the dead.'" (TLB)

Pretty plain, huh?
Yeah. I don't like that.
I'm glad. You *shouldn't* like it. Hell is not going to be a big party.
But I hear my non-Christian friends joke and say they're all going to

hell together. They laugh about all the stuff they're gonna do with no one to stop them.

The truth is, people won't even recognize each other in hell. You can't imagine how tremendously painful it will be to burn forever in flames of fire that can't be extinguished—and never have relief. It's *not* going to be party time!

Wow. That sounds so strong.

Yes, it does. And remember that every time hell is mentioned in the Bible, I've used strong language to describe it.

Guess that's because You want to make sure we stay away from it, huh?

Exactly.

You know, Father, I hear the word *hell* a lot. I mean, kids at school toss it around so casually. Is that right?

No. They're using it as a cuss word. They've reduced an actual place to a mere slang term. And you're right, it's a word you hear often—on TV, in the hallways, at work—but again, remember the *truth.* Hell is not simply an expression to use when you're angry. It's an actual *place* where people who don't know Me will spend eternity.

Whew! That's strong.

Yes. Hell is heavy. It's not a laughing matter. Know what else is heavy?

What?

Millions around you are dying spiritually. They're searching for answers, for truth, and for peace. You have the answer. You know the Truth, because you know Me. Many of your friends are headed for hell, and it's up to you to point them in the right direction.

I usually don't think about it that seriously. I mean, I know the kids at my school who aren't Christians, but it's usually pretty easy to just shrug it off. After all, if they wanna party and mess around, I can't stop 'em.

But the reason they're partying and messing around is because they're seriously searching for some answers—for peace, for joy.

Think they even realize they're searching for something?

Probably not. But it's obvious, isn't it?

Yeah.

And the heavy part is, *you* have the answer. *You* can make a difference in their lives. *You* can help point them in the right direction!

Yeah, I *want* to—I really do. I . . . . I'm just scared. (But don't tell anyone I said that!)

Hey, this is just between you and Me, okay?

Okay. Good.

It's okay to be scared.

It is?

Sure! That's normal.

Whew! Feels good to be normal.

Everyone's a little nervous when it comes to talking about his or her faith.

Yeah! Because my relationship with You is a personal thing. I mean, it's so important to me that I'm always struggling even to put it into words.

I understand. But that's where I come in.

Whaddya mean?

I'll provide the words you need.

That's a relief; but I'm still scared.

And you *will* be. Remember how frightened you were the first time you tried downhill skiing?

Oh, man! I'll never forget that. I stood at the top of that mountain, looked down, and thought my life was over!

But after you did it a few times, you started to enjoy it.

Yeah. I took quite a few spills that first day.

And even a few the next several trips too.

Okay. Okay. We can skip over my bad ski days!

All right. I'm wrapping it up. Here's the lesson: The more you skied, the more comfortable you became with it. Yes, you took some bad spills, but you got over them. Now you even look *forward* to those ski trips with family and friends.

That's right! So, You're saying the more I fall on my face with my non-Christian friends, the more comfortable I'll be with making a fool outta myself?

Partly.

What?

I'm saying the more you share your faith, the more confident you'll become in doing it. And yes . . . after you stutter around a few times, you'll become better and better at it. Finally, it can become second nature to you.

That's hard to believe!

Hard to believe if you're doing it on your own.

But easier to swallow since I know You really *are* in charge.

Exactly.

God, I really don't want any of my friends to go to hell.

I don't either. I *died* for your friends.

It sounds worse than a nightmare.

It is, My child. And the worst part?

Yeah?

Is eternal separation from Me.

Yeah.

You see . . . once you're in heaven, that's it. I mean, it's not like you're going to get close to the edge and accidentally fall out or anything.

Yeah, I know that.

But on the same thought, once you're in hell, that's it. You're there to stay. You're not going to get another chance. No other options. You won't be able to renegotiate.

That's frightening. I mean . . . we all think we have a million chances.

You know: "I don't have to get my act together yet. I'll have fun first, *then* give my life to Christ." It's as though we think time will never run out.

Yes, that's exactly what many of your friends are thinking.

I wanna help them, God. I really do. But I'm still pretty nervous about it.

That's okay. We'll start small.

How?

First of all, let's start with your life. Let Me help you remove those things that keep Me from shining through you as brightly as I can.

Like what?

We'll start with some of the movies you're watching.

Oh.

We'll use your *life* as a silent witness.

All right.

And I'll begin working in Chad's heart. I can soften a heart like nobody's business.

Then what?

Once Chad's heart begins to soften, he'll begin noticing the difference in your life.

Yeah?

Yeah.

Then what?

Then he's going to start asking questions.

Like what?

Like what makes your life so different?

And then?

By that time, your youth group will be having its winter retreat.

Oh, yeah! I forgot about that. Cool!

And I'll remind you to invite him.

And then what?

He'll have lots of questions for you at the retreat. He'll hear My

message of salvation. And he'll realize he's missing something in his life.

And that's when I start telling him about You?

Exactly.

But what'll I say?

I'll give you the words, My child.

I trust You, Father.

And by that time, you'll be so anxious to tell him about Me, you'll hardly be able to wait until he asks the questions.

Think so?

I know so.

Why? Why will I be so anxious to tell him about You?

Because I'd like you to start praying for him.

All right.

And when you pray diligently for someone, you become burdened for him. And I'm able to *increase* the burden for that person every time you pray.

I will, Father. I will. I'll start right now. I don't want Chad to end up in hell. And if You can use *me* to make a difference, well . . . You go, God!

It's *that* kind of willing attitude, My child, that will enable Me to reach *this* generation!

On Eating Disorders

God said: You're not eating it.

I said: I know.

But your pastor said the words. He's prayed. He's given direction.

I know Communion is special, Lord.

More than special. It's sacred.

I know.

And you're not eating the bread.

I can't. I just can't do it.

My child, you're forgiven.

I know, Jesus. But I can't eat it.

Why?

You know why, Lord. You know everything.

Yes, but we still need to talk about it. You need to voice your feelings to Me.

I don't want to. I'm scared.

I know. But you're not alone.

I'm still scared.

Come here, My child. Sit in My lap. Cry on My shoulder.

Oh, Jesus!

I want to share Communion with you.

I know.

It's My sacred covenant. The breaking of My very body.

I know, Jesus. I didn't want to cry.

It's okay. Tears are the beginning of healing.

You won't make me eat the bread, will You?

No. But you need to tell Me why you're not participating in Communion.

I'm scared, Lord. I'm so scared of the calories.

I know.

I hate this . . . this monster within me.

I hate it too.

It's a constant battle of calories and fat grams and throwing up and exercising till my joints are swollen.

An eating disorder is a monster that can eventually kill you.

I know. But I can't help it.

***You* can't help yourself. But *I* can help you.**

I'm too scared to let You help me.

Why?

I'm afraid You'll make me eat. And that will cause me to gain weight.

Let's forget about food for a while.

Forget about it? I'm obsessed with it! It's always on my mind—when I go to bed at night, when I wake up in the wee hours of the morning, and when I crawl outta bed to the sound of my alarm clock. I never stop thinking about it. How can we "forget about it for a while"?

I want you to concentrate on something else.

Why? If You really want to help me, Jesus, You'll start with my battle with food.

No, I'll start at the beginning.

The beginning?

The issue is never food, My child.

What issue? I just want a great body!

The issue always goes much deeper.

I don't know anything about an issue, Lord. All I know is how scared I am to gain weight.

I know, My child. I know.

It terrifies me.

Will you allow Me to take you past the surface?

Whaddya mean?

Let's find the issue *together.*

No.

No?

I'm too scared.

Of what we'll find?

Of what we won't. What if there's nothing to find? No underlying message? No hidden meaning. No answer.

There's always an answer. In fact, *I* can be your answer. But I need to guide you to some things you've intentionally blocked out.

Why?

Why I need to guide you there? Because that's where healing will begin. Why you've intentionally blocked them out? Because you're hurting.

Thanks for understanding.

I do, My child. And I love you so much!

Even if I gain too much weight?

I love you *agape.*

A-what-a?

A-gop-ay. It's Greek. It means "I love you." Period. No matter what. No stipulations. No expectations. Not if. Not when. Not because. Just "I love you." And that's always and forever . . . as in eternal.

Oh, Jesus! That feels so good. I don't deserve it, but I sure am grateful for it. I'm sorry I can't stop crying.

That's all right, My child. I'll wipe your tears as long as you cry. In fact . . . I'll even cry *with* you.

Why would You do that?

Because when you hurt, I hurt.

Can we leave church, Jesus? I'd rather not sit here while everyone else is taking Communion. Can we go someplace private?

Anywhere you feel comfortable.

This is much better.

There's no place like home.

Home, sweet home.

Sit down. Let's talk this thing through.

Okay. Well, I'm not sure where to begin, but I feel so trapped. I feel lost. Hopeless. Like I've fallen into a deep, deep hole and there's no one offering me a rope. I'm so alone.

I'm in the hole with you. And I offer My body as the ladder you need to crawl out.

But I'm scared to crawl out, Jesus! I *want* outta the hole . . . but I'm scared!

I know. That's why we're going to back up.

Where?

Well, let's get a good, close look at the hole.

What are You talking about?

Trust Me.

I'll try.

Look around. Describe the hole you're in.

It's filled with pressure—all kinds of expectations. I am so acutely aware of my aloneness. And even though I'm the only one living here, I'm not in charge of the decorations.

Who is?

I'm not sure. I just know I'm not in charge.

How do you feel about that?

Angry. Desperate. Like I wanna "show 'em."

Whom do you want to show?

I don't know.

Look around. Who decorated this hole?

Uh . . . well. I've never taken time to notice. But, well . . . I see a picture hung over the fireplace by my mom.

What is it?

It's a picture of me.

Describe it.

I'm twelve years old.

What else?

I'm wearing my Easter dress. She made it for me. I got to pick out the material and everything. I was so excited.

I remember.

We even got shoes to match the light pink in the trim.

Yes?

I can't. I hate this—remembering. I don't want to talk anymore, Jesus.

But I do. And the more you hurt, the tighter I'll hug, okay?

Well . . . when she was making the dress, I remember how frustrated she got . . . because it wouldn't fit. She had to let it out. She said I had gained weight, and if I wasn't careful I'd get fat . . . and that people would wonder why I couldn't control myself.

I'm so sorry.

Oh, Jesus! I haven't thought of that in years.

Not consciously. But it's been in your subconscious—eating you alive, tormenting you.

Why'd she say that, Lord? I mean . . . she wouldn't lie to me. It must have been true!

Oh, My child. You were at an awkward age: You were right at the beginning of puberty—the time when your body is *supposed* to

change shape and size. You see, I designed it so that your hips would begin to widen and your—

Why? Why would You do that, Jesus?

It's all part of the plan. You see, I've designed women to have wider hips than men, because of the birthing process. Women *need* wider hips to give birth. It was never meant to make you self-conscious, but to help you when delivering a brand-new creation.

Well, when You put it that way, it doesn't sound so bad.

It's *not* bad. It's My plan. It's *normal*.

Then why did Mom make such a big deal out of it?

Because she was insecure.

Why?

Because of some things that happened to her when she was growing up.

Like what?

We'll deal with those issues at a later time. Right now, let's stick with you. You're in a hole. You're fighting a battle you will *not* win on your own. You need to get out.

I *want* out, Jesus. And if hips aren't that big of a deal, I don't want to be obsessed about them.

Good. Now keep telling Me about your hole. What else do you see?

Um. Well . . . I see my fourteenth birthday party. There's the picture—right over there. It's on my bulletin board.

Tell Me about it.

We're sitting around the picnic table in our backyard: Me, Cassandra, Josh, Evan, Kacie, Amanda, and Shayla. See the birthday cake?

Yes. It looks great!

It was.

And all the presents.

Yeah. Kacie gave me some really cool stationery. And Evan gave me a goldfish. I can't remember what everyone else brought, but it was great.

You're not smiling.

Yes, I am. See?

You were smiling on the *outside*, but that's not what I'm talking about. I can see way past a smile. I can see your heart in this picture. And it's breaking.

Yeah.

Why?

Ah, I don't know. I probably didn't get the gift I wanted.

No. That's not why you aren't smiling.

Since You're God . . . and since You already know everything, why do we have to talk about it?

Because this is where healing begins. We need to look at the hurt.

Well, notice Dad in the background?

Yes.

He's flippin' burgers on the grill. They had cheese and everything.

Must have been good.

They were great.

But it wasn't the burgers that broke your heart.

No. It was what Mom said.

Keep going.

Well, she had made fries to go with the burgers.

Yes.

And we had homemade ice cream and dill pickles and baked beans.

Yes.

But my favorite was the fries. And when they were passed to me, she reached over my head—she was standing behind me—and passed them on to Amanda, who was sitting next to me. Mom said, "You don't need fries *and* cake, and since you're the birthday girl, you *have* to have cake. So pass the fries on to Amanda."

I'm sorry. I'm so sorry.

I was humiliated, Jesus. Everyone was eating fries! Why'd she even make them if it was wrong for me to eat them?

It wasn't wrong. But unfortunately you got a wrong message.

She might as well have grabbed a microphone and announced, "My daughter is fat. She can't have the fries. She weighs too much."

But you didn't weigh too much.

But that's what I heard.

It was a false message. Again, you were at the age when *all* girls' bodies are changing. Your metabolism, your hormones, your shifting weight—it's normal for all of that to change. Physically, that's what growing up is all about.

It still hurts as though she'd said it yesterday.

I know.

I'm eighteen now, Jesus. And it still hurts.

Let's remove the picture.

We can't do that.

Why not?

Mom hung it there.

It's okay. I'm redecorating. Will you give it to Me?

Never to look at again?

You'll still remember it, but it doesn't need to be hanging on your wall in full display breaking your heart all over again every time you glance toward that wall. I can heal that hurt. Give it up.

You can have it, Jesus.

Keep going. What else is in your hole?

Well, there's my report card.

Which one?

Third grade. See it? It's hanging on the fridge next to Jason's construction-paper dinosaur.

I see it. You did great! Three As, a B, and a B-minus.

I was so proud of that card. That's the year we started multiplication and division. I really struggled with it.

I remember.

I couldn't believe I got a B-minus. I just knew I was headed toward a C . . . or maybe even a D.

But you worked really hard those last two weeks.

Yeah.

And you did it! You brought home a B-minus! I was so proud of you.

Yeah, but Dad wasn't.

Keep going.

He said he just couldn't understand why my grades were so unpredictable. Why I didn't bring home all As. He said I just wasn't trying hard enough. That I daydreamed too much. And that if I'd only apply myself, I could do better.

I'm sorry. My child.

I thought I *did* do better.

You did. You did great!

Then why did Dad say that? And why did I feel so guilty?

You've been carrying around false guilt.

False guilt?

Right. There was no reason in the world for you to feel bad about your grades. You did a super job! But because of what your dad said to you, you began to feel guilty when you shouldn't have. False guilt.

False guilt.

Give it up.

I don't think I can just disintegrate it. I need to put it somewhere.

I'll hold it.

But—

If you ever need false guilt again . . . we'll know where to find it.

What will I need it for?

You won't. It's My desire that you *never* experience false guilt for the rest of your life.

Then why'd You say we'll know where to find it if I need it?

I was kidding. I'm trying to help you realize how silly it is to think that you can't get rid of it forever. I have the power to disintegrate

that false guilt. We don't need to keep it on the shelf. It's not really something you need to have in storage.

Oh.

But you're afraid to give it up completely, because you're used to leaning on it.

Leaning on it?

It's become a crutch.

Yeah. You're right. Go ahead, Jesus. Take that false guilt. Here—I'm giving You my third-grade report card.

Thank you, My child. I'll destroy it.

All right.

Look around you. What do you see?

Walls. Cracked walls. Bruised walls. Tear-stained walls. But . . . hey! The walls are empty! There are no more pictures in the hole.

That's right. We're redecorating.

I already feel a sense of freedom I've never felt before.

My child, think about the pictures and mementos you've given Me: The photo of your Easter dress when you were twelve.

Boy, it sure feels good not to have *that* hanging around anymore.

And your fourteenth birthday party.

Something inside me is still screaming for fries . . . but scared to death to eat them.

And your third-grade report card.

Are You sure I did well, Jesus? Maybe I *could* have done better in arithmetic.

You did great, My child—I promise. But take a long look at each of these keepsakes, because I'm getting ready to toss them very far away. You'll remember them, but though it will be a process, you'll eventually not be obsessing over them any longer. But first, as you look at each of them, can you see how your feelings of being trapped began to develop?

No. I don't get it.

Your mom placed unreal expectations on you. She expected you to remain at an impossible little-girl weight, when your body was designed to gain and grow and develop.

Oh.

And she was so focused on what she wanted you to become physically, she wasn't able to notice the damage she was doing to your heart.

Yeah.

And your dad expected you to bring home perfect grades. He forgot that little girls are supposed to play in sand boxes, climb trees, and ride bicycles as well as do homework.

Yeah. I would've given anything to roller blade after school. Instead, I was afraid I'd disappoint him if I wasn't studying when he got home.

I know. Can you see how all that has made you feel trapped?

Maybe.

You've felt like everyone else has had a say in your life and how you should live it—except you.

Yeah! That's exactly how I've felt.

And the only thing you *could* control was your weight, right?

Right!

But I don't even want you to control *that.*

What?

I want you to give *Me* control of your weight.

But—

And not just your weight . . . but your obsession with gaining, the feeling of having to measure up, your perfectionism, your fear of disappointing someone, your bingeing, your laxatives, your throwing up food, your future, your dreams, your everything.

But Jesus . . . You already live inside my heart. Don't You remember when I became a Christian? It was at Vacation Bible School in fourth grade.

Oh, I remember. All of heaven rejoiced that day.

So what are You talking about?

I've lived inside your heart. I've been a part of your life. But I want total control. I want to *be* your life.

But what does food have to do with Christianity?

Anything you refuse to give Me has everything to do with Christianity.

We're talking about Lordship, aren't we?

Right.

But what if I gain weight?

Do you want out of the hole?

Yes.

Trust Me.

But what if I gain weight?

Do you trust Me?

Maybe. I mean . . . I trust You with my future career. And I trust You with my dating life. But my *weight*?

Lordship means everything.

Yeah, but what if I gain?

Do you want out of the hole?

We've been here before.

And we'll keep going over and over the same ground, until you get it. I love you, My child. I love you beyond your highest dreams. Trust Me!

I want outta the hole, Lord.

I created your body. I know exactly how it works. Will you trust Me with My physical design for you?

Yeah.

Good.

But what if I gain weight?

NMW.

NMW?

No matter what, remember? I love you NO MATTER WHAT.

Yeah, You'll still love me . . . because You *have* to. But You won't love me quite as much. I know it, Jesus. I know it.

I love you because I *want* to—not because I have to. I'm God. I don't *have* to do anything. But I love you so much I willingly went through an indescribable death for you. I LOVE you, My child. I *love* you! And no, I'll *never* love you any less.

You won't?

My child, there is absolutely *nothing* you can do that will ever cause Me to love you more than I do right now. I'm bursting with love for you! You can read the Bible from start to finish four times a year, and it won't make Me love you any more than I do right now.

Wow! But don't get Your hopes up about that four times a year thing.

But at the same time, I want you to know that there's nothing—NOTH-ING—you could ever do that would cause Me to love you any less.

Nothing?

Nothing.

Really nothing?

Really, absolutely nothing.

Nada?

Zip.

Zilch?

I think you get the picture.

So . . . if I gain weight?

NMW—no matter what.

And if my grades slip at the university?

NMW.

No matter what.

You've got it!

Wow. Jesus, do You have any idea how secure this makes me feel?

Yes, I'm God. I know exactly how you feel.

I feel so safe!

Yes! That's exactly how I *want* you to feel!

And I feel so loved!

Yes!

And . . .

Beautiful?

Well . . .

You *are*, you know. You're a creation of the King. I made you in love and with great care. I'm so proud of how you turned out. You are *soooo* loved.

Yes! I *do* feel beautiful.

It's time.

Time?

To crawl out of this hole.

I'm ready, Lord.

Take My hand. We're headed for new heights.

Hey! I almost forgot what fresh air smells like. This is great!

I want you to do something.

What?

I want you to keep talking to Me about all this.

Why?

Because your healing isn't finished. It's going to be a process. That means it's going to take time.

I'll keep talking with You, Jesus. You have complete control of my life. You are Lord.

I want you to talk with someone else too.

Who?

We'll find her. I want to direct you to a godly counselor—someone who can walk *with* us through this process.

You're not dumping me off on someone, are You?

No way! I'm in this for the long haul. I paid too great a price for you to simply leave you halfway. NMW, remember?

Yeah. NMW!

Ready to go?

Well . . . there's one more thing I'd like to do.

What's that?

I'd like to take Communion. But I'm afraid it's too late.

It's never too late.

Sure it is. We're not even in church anymore.

Yes we are.

Huh?

Church is wherever you worship Me.

You mean . . . right here?

Right now.

Yeah, I guess. But I'm really sorry I turned down Communion because I was obsessing over the calories in the bread.

It's okay. We can have our own.

We can?

Sure. I'd break My body a million more times—and give it away in love each time—just for you.

No, Jesus.

Yes, My child. I love you.

Oh, Jesus! I love You too. And I trust You. I really do. *I trust You, Lord!*

Take this bread.

I take this bread.

It symbolizes My body.

It symbolizes Your body.

Which is broken . . .

Which is broken . . .

. . . and freely given . . .

. . . and freely given . . .

. . . to you, My beloved child.

. . . to me. From my Hero. My Abba. My Savior. My GOD.

Amen.

NMW.

God understands. He really does. He knows about your personal struggles, and He died to give you the power to overcome them. If you're battling an eating disorder, have you given it to Him? He wants it! He wants to walk you through a healing process that will change your mind *and* your self-image.

How about right now? Will you take a moment to explain your struggle to God? Tell Him everything—your hurt, your confusion, your fear. Lay it down. Give it away. Ask Him to guide your healing process. He may lead you to a Christian counselor. He may direct you to a check-in facility. Be willing to follow His lead. He cares more about your wholeness than even you do!

We often erect walls when we're hurt. Sometimes those walls take the shape of an eating disorder, sometimes they take the shape of bitterness and an unforgiving spirit. God wants to give you the strength to gently tear down those walls in His power. As you read the next conversation, ask God if there are any walls of unforgiveness in your life that need to come down. Then be willing to join His demolition crew.

11

On Forgiveness

God said: You miss her, don't you?

I said: Alison?

Yes.

Ah, not really.

Hm. Not even walking to school together?

Nah. It's kind of nice being alone. Gives me time to think.

Not even having lunch together in the school cafeteria?

It's probably better that I eat faster anyway; it gives me time to leave and get started on my homework.

And what about youth group?

Well, I'm still going to Sunday school. I guess it's not that important that I go to youth group all the time. I wouldn't want to go and be there with Alison. It would feel too awkward.

Isn't it awkward *now*—holding this grudge against her?

Well . . . yeah . . . things are weird. But . . . it would be even *weirder* to forgive her.

Or would it?

Huh?

Just how long do you plan on trying to avoid her? Eating alone. Hanging out by yourself. Missing youth group. Wouldn't it be easier to simply forgive her and get on with your life?

No.

Are you sure?

Positive.

Hm. Remember the time you lied to your mom about breaking your curfew?

That was over a year ago! You sure have a good memory.

I'm God. I know everything.

Oh, yeah. Okay, so what's the deal? Why are You suddenly changing the subject from Alison to my curfew? That has absolutely nothing to do with how she hurt me.

The point is, you lied. But I forgave you.

Well, that wasn't hard to forgive. It was only curfew!

My child, any time you lie, you're being deceptive—and that goes directly against My holy character. It hurts Me.

Hurts You? Nah. Murder—that hurts You. And children starving. That's gotta hurt. And Your heart probably breaks every time someone is abused. But stretching the truth about curfew? Nah, that can't hurt.

When you lie, My child, you're breaking one of the Ten Commandments. You're going directly against My plan for your life. You're sinning. Every sin—murder, abuse, stealing, gossip, lying—they *all* hurt Me. And they hurt deeply. I *died* so that you wouldn't have to pay the penalty for those sins.

I'm sorry, Lord. I guess I just wasn't thinking that stretching the truth about my curfew was really a sin. But, You're right. *Any* time I choose to deceive someone, I'm lying. I'm so sorry, Jesus.

I know you are. I know your heart. It's tender. I have forgiven you.

Whew! That sure feels good.

But we're not finished.

Well, yeah we are. You know I'm sorry. And I've accepted Your for-giveness.

But we're still not finished. What about Alison?

Oh, man! Why did You have to bring *her* up again?

Because she's My child, and I love her deeply. I died for her too, you know.

But, Lord! She really hurt me. She *really* hurt me! I mean . . . You have no idea.

Oh, I know all about hurt. Two of My own disciples betrayed Me. One sold Me for a lousy thirty pieces of silver. My *life* for thirty pieces of silver! And the other one—one whom I had nicknamed "the Rock" and said I'd build My church on—lied and said he didn't know Me—had never even heard of Me. Yes, My child, I know all about hurt.

Yeah, but Judas was a weirdo from the very beginning. Alison's not a weirdo. What I'm going through doesn't even compare to a couple of disciples—especially since Peter got back on good terms with You, and Judas was such a flake.

Flake? Weirdo? The day before I selected My twelve disciples, I had spent the entire night praying about whom to choose. None of them were chosen flippantly. Judas was chosen to follow Me because he was stacked with talent and ability. He showed prom-ise and possessed such an eagerness. He wasn't weird. He was good with numbers. He was dependable. The other disciples trusted him enough to put him in charge of our financial funds. Yes, he eventually betrayed Me, but it didn't happen overnight. He slowly began backing away emotionally and spiritually before he ever made his physical move of betrayal. I know about hurt.

Yeah, but it all turned out okay.

Okay?

Well, yeah. I mean, he killed himself. So You never had to think about it again. I'm always running into Alison, and the hurt is fresh every time I see her!

My heart broke for Judas. If only he would have sought Me out before hanging himself. If only he would have found Me.

Why? What difference would that have made?

A lot. You see, My child, I would have forgiven him—if only he would have asked.

Forgiven him? *Forgiven him?* He betrayed You, Lord! How could You have forgiven him?

He's not the only one who has betrayed Me.

Well, yeah . . . Peter. But he sought forgiveness.

Peter and Judas aren't the ones I'm thinking of right now.

Well, who else, Jesus?

You, My child.

Me?!?

You.

Oh, Jesus! Please don't say that! I'd never betray You.

When you refuse to forgive someone who has hurt you, you're betraying Me.

No!

I want you to forgive Alison.

I can't, Lord! It hurts too much!

I understand. I know all about hurt. And when *you* hurt, I hurt. I've cried the tears with you. You've never been alone.

But, God, it's just not fair! She promised she'd never tell anyone. I trusted her. I wouldn't tell just *anyone* who I like. And she gave me her word she'd never tell. Then she had to go and blab it to Justin that I think he's hot. How could she? I've never been so embarrassed in my entire life!

I understand. I created you, and I know how badly your heart is bruised right now. But, I promise . . . it's not the end of the world.

It sure feels like it!

And there's more to the story than Alison simply breaking her promise to you.

What?!?

She was trying to get Justin to ask you to the cookout next week.

What?!?

She thought if he knew you liked him, he'd have the confidence he needed to ask you.

What?!?

It's true.

Well . . . what . . . she . . . I mean . . . how . . .

She *did* break a promise—and I know you're hurting over that. And she *did* tell Justin something that you're wishing he didn't know. But she didn't do it out of spite. Believe it or not, she was trying to help. Granted, she didn't think it through. Yes, she should have talked it over with you—asked your permission. But she wasn't out to hurt you. That was not her motive.

I never knew.

Because you never asked.

She should have told me.

She tried. But it's hard to hear when you're running away while she's talking.

Well . . . I didn't know.

You reacted out of hurt, instead of expecting the best of her.

It still hurts.

I know.

And I'm still embarrassed.

I realize that. But if I can forgive those who have wronged *Me*, shouldn't you also forgive those who break your trust?

Yeah, probably.

Could you be a little more definite?

But I'm still angry! And I don't think it's fair that I should have to forgive her. After all, she *did* promise. She broke her promise, Lord!

And I know your hurt. But the bottom line is this: You'll break one of your promises to Me sometime in the next couple of weeks. Should I forgive you?

Well, sure, Jesus! You know my heart. You know I love You. And yeah, sometimes I blow it. But my relationship with You is important to me. I always ask You for forgiveness when I know I've gone against Your will.

My child . . . if you don't forgive those who hurt you, it stands in the way of *My* bestowing forgiveness upon *you*.

But, Jesus! You can't hold this against me! Alison hurt me.

And you'll hurt *Me*.

You've gotta forgive me when I blow it. I'm just sixteen! I don't always realize I'm even *doing* something that hurts You until I'm right in the middle of doing it. But I'm always sorry!

I know you are. I know your heart.

Okay, then.

But I also know Alison's heart. And I know that she's sorry about the embarrassment she's caused you. She loves you. She treasures your friendship. You two have a lot of great memories together. I want you to forgive her. By extending your forgiveness to her, it keeps your heart uncluttered and allows My forgiveness to flow freely to *you*.

Wow. I never thought of it that way before. It's really pretty complicated, isn't it?

No, not really.

Well, it *sounds* complicated.

It's simply a decision to allow Me to be Lord of your life. Not just of your future, your talents, your family. But allowing Me to forgive others through you—letting Me be the Lord of your hurt too.

I think I'm getting it, Jesus. But I still don't think it's fair. I mean, she *did* hurt me!

Forgiveness isn't always fair, My child. But it's always right.
And sometimes it hurts to do the right thing.

You *are* getting it!

Well, to be honest . . . I *am* pretty tired of carrying this grudge around. I really miss my friendship with Alison. I think I'll go call her. I'm gonna need a ride to youth group tonight.

And you're also going to need a ride for Saturday.

Saturday?

That barbecue. The cookout at church.

Nah. I don't think I wanna go. I'd be too uncomfortable around Justin.

First dates usually *are* a little uncomfortable.

First dates?

Justin.

You mean—

Yes.

Oh, my goodness! I'd better run to the mall. I don't have anything to wear! I've gotta get moving! I'll buy those khakis I saw marked down half-price, and I might be able to get—

I wouldn't go just yet.

Why not?

Because before you'll even have time to get to the mall, your phone will be ringing.

Justin?!?! How do You know? I mean, how can You—

Trust Me. I'm God.

You're right. I'll sit right here, Lord. I'll stay right next to the phone, and I won't pick it up until he calls.

No. Go ahead and pick it up. There's someone *you* need to call, remember? She needs your forgiveness.

Oh, yeah. And maybe there's something else I should give her.

Yes?

A huge apology.

You really *are* getting it, aren't you?

Well . . . I *do* have a great Teacher.

I love you, My child.   ✳

Thanks. And Jesus?

Yes?

Thanks, too, for being patient enough to keep on with me until I finally get it.

12

On Reaching Out

God said: What about Julianna?

I said: What about her?

Why does she always eat lunch alone?

I don't know.

Have you ever thought about it?

Not really.

Why not?

Well, that's just her. I mean . . . she *always* eats alone. I guess I'm just used to seeing her in the school cafeteria by herself.

Hm.

It's no big deal. She probably likes it.

Would *you* like it?

No way! I'm too much of a people-person to hang out by myself at lunch time!

Yet you'd have to . . . if no one chose to sit with you.

Whaddya mean if no one chose to sit with me? I've always got a *few* friends I can count on!

But what if you didn't?

C'mon, God. What are You getting at?

Think about it: What if you really *wanted* to be with people but you couldn't find anyone to sit with you at lunch?

No one?

No one.

Well, that'd be pretty tough. I mean . . . I . . . I'd really be hurting inside. I'd probably go home and cry every day.

Good.

Good?!?

Good—now you're thinking outside of yourself.

Whaddya mean?

You're imagining how someone else might feel if she were all alone but didn't really want to be.

You mean . . . Julianna?

Right.

Well, that's different. *She's* different.

How is she different?

Well, for one thing, she's always alone.

I thought we already covered this.

Well, what are You trying to say, God?

Okay. Yes, she's alone. We've already established that fact. But *could* it be that she doesn't really *want* to be alone?

I don't know. I just always assumed she wanted it that way or she'd do something about it.

Hm. Remember when you first started riding the bus to school?

Yeah. That was third grade.

Right.

5o?

You didn't know anyone on the bus. You sat with a different kid every day—hoping to make a friend—but they ignored you simply because you were the new "bus kid."

I forgot all about that. Man! That was really a hard year.

Yes, it was . . . until February.

February?

It was February 3 that your older sister asked her friend Julie to consider *not* driving her little sister, Marcie, to school. She knew that you and Marcie were good friends and if Marcie would ride the bus with you, you'd be more comfortable.

Hey! I never knew Lindsay did that!

She loves you.

Lindsay asked Julie to encourage Marcie to ride my bus?

That's right. And since you only lived three blocks away from each other, Lindsay knew you'd both have the same route.

Wow. I'm really glad Lindsay did that, because Marcie and I had a great time on the bus! It felt *soooo* good to finally have a friend to ride with me. You know, someone to laugh with, talk with, *be* with.

Now back to Julianna.

Well, I don't ride the bus anymore.

I know. But the same principle is at work here.

You've lost me, God.

Think about it. You really *wanted* someone to sit with on the bus. But it never happened until someone else stepped in and helped you with the friendship you needed.

Yeah.

So never assume that just because someone's alone it's her choice. Maybe Julianna doesn't know *how* to do anything about it. If you needed help, maybe she could use some help too.

Okay, so what are You saying, God? Give it to me straight.

I want you to eat lunch with her.

You're kidding, right?

No. I was kidding when I gave the hyenas laughter. But I'm not kidding about Julianna needing a friend.

But what about *my* friends?

What about them?

I can't just leave them!

I didn't ask you to.

But You want me to eat lunch with Julianna! How can I just ignore my friends—the girls I eat with every single day—to go sit with a loner?

You don't have to leave them. Invite Julianna to eat at *your* table.

Oh, man!

Remember how hurt you were back in third grade?

Yeah.

Julianna's hurting. My child. I care about her. I need *you* to reach out to her.

But what'll I say?

Don't worry about that. I'll give you the words.

And what if she turns me down?

Don't worry about that, either. I've already started preparing her heart.

What do You mean?

Well . . . she's been praying for a friend.

You're kidding?!!

No. That was the hyenas, remember?

Oh, yeah. But God . . . You mean . . . she's a Christian?

That's right. And she's been praying for three months that I'd help her find another Christian friend at this school.

Wow. I never knew.

I've been trying to speak to you.

You mean . . . all that stuff my youth leader's been saying about bringing someone to church?

Yes.

And loving someone new?

Yes.

And those Sunday school lessons on not excluding others?

Yes.

And Mom asking me if I've made any new friends this year?

Yes.

Man! I sure am hard-headed sometimes. I'm sorry, Father. All this time, I've been praying that You'd use me in a special way this year at school. And Julianna's been right under my nose the whole time! Why didn't I think of this on my own?

You were *praying* for an opportunity . . . but you weren't *looking* for an opportunity. There's a difference.

Yeah! A big difference.

When you ask Me to use you, always expect that I'll bring an opportunity your way to do just that.

Father, I *want* to be used.

I know, My child.

I *want* You to make a difference through me.

I will. But you've got to make the first move. YOU reach out . . . and trust ME to do the rest.

Father, will You forgive me for being so blinded to the needs of those around me? I'm really sorry.

You're forgiven. And with a tender heart like that, I can use you in numerous ways this year.

Thanks, Father. I gotta go now.

Where are you going?

I'm gonna call Amber and Kelli and Emily and Kristine and remind them that You want to use us to make a difference in Julianna's life.

Great! I'll come with you.

On Sex

*S*exual purity. You've heard that term so much, you may be tired of talking about it. But even though it's tossed around a lot, what *is* it? Does sexual purity mean the same thing as virginity? Well, yes. I mean, no. Hm. Just go ahead and dive into this next conversation. I think it'll clear up a few things. We'll chat again after the conversation, okay?

I said: Where's that CD?

God said: Next to your jeans.

I just saw it two days ago.

Underneath your university sweatshirt.

Never can find anything when I need it.

On top of the pillow on your bed.

Ugh!

You're ignoring Me.

I'll bet Lacey took it.

Listen to Me.

She's always sneaking into my room and borrowing my stuff!

I'm talking to you.

Kid sisters!

If you'll stop long enough to listen, you'll hear Me.

Lacey!

I'm waiting.

My chemistry book. Notebook. Backpack. Hair clips. Purple nail polish. Pillow.

Jeans.

Jeans.

University sweatshirt.

University sweatshirt.

CD.

Ah! Here it is!

Now that you've got what you want, how 'bout listening to Me for a few minutes?

Hey, there's my Student Bible. Sheesh! Haven't seen *that* in a while. In fact . . . wow. I haven't picked this up since . . . well, since Jarod and I started dating. Whew, this is dusty! Oh yeah, here's my bookmark from camp. Wow, what a week *that* was! God was so close then.

And I'm yearning to be close again.

But He seems so far away now.

I'm as close as your heart.

And I don't really *feel* Him anymore.

You don't really *pray* anymore.

Sigh. Seems like forever since we've talked.

Yes. Think about it. Why have you stopped talking with Me?

Ah . . . those camp days. Everything seemed so simple then.

Jarod wasn't in the picture.

But since Jarod and I started dating . . . I don't know. It's like I'm not as free to talk about stuff with God like I used to.

Think about it. Come on.

Ah, what am I doing sitting around reminiscing?

No, don't stop. I'm trying to get through.

It's just that . . . well . . . hey! Here's my memory verse—all high-lighted in fluorescent yellow—James 4:28.

Yes! Come on. I'm *yearning* to be with you.

Wow. A lot sure has happened since camp. Well . . . a lot's happened since Jarod and I got together.

Keep on. You're getting close. Talk to Me.

Sigh. I miss the intimacy God and I used to have.

No. Not third person. It's Me! Direct your thoughts to Me—first person. Come on!

There was a time I couldn't wait to open the Bible and read His words.

You're getting closer . . . not *His* words . . . *My* words.

I told Him everything. Hey, what is this? Why am I getting so sappy? I found the CD I was looking for. Lacey didn't take it after all. I guess just flipping through my Student Bible is bringing back so many memories. I don't know . . . I feel sad. Distanced. Alone.

You're never alone. I'm right here.

Sigh. Oh, God. What happened?

YES! Finally. We're talking. I love you, My child.

God?

Yes! It's Me.

God?!? I can't believe it. You're here!

I never left.

Why have You been so distant?

I haven't. I've been right here the whole time.

But I haven't felt close to You.

You haven't *been* close to Me.

But . . . You just said You never left.

I didn't. *You* did.

Well, Father, I . . . ah, I don't know.

Yes, you do.

Yeah. Okay. Well, I just haven't felt comfortable enough to talk with You. Something's changed.

Yes. Something *has* changed. Disobedience will do that. It places distance between us. Remember Adam and Eve? They tried to hide from Me. They disobeyed, and they felt distant because of it.

Is disobedience the only thing that causes distance?

No. Guilt will cause it too.

Guilt.

Guilt from disobedience.

I'm striking out, aren't I?

Talk to Me.

Well . . . uh . . . okay. So. Um . . . hey, this is weird. I don't know what to say. It's been too long.

It's never too long.

Well, I'm just not comfortable talking to You anymore.

I know. That's why we need to talk.

So how come You don't like Jarod?

I love Jarod. I *died* for him. In fact . . . if he were the only person in the entire world, I still would have gone to all the trouble to create it just as beautiful as it is.

Huh?

Think about it. The Grand Canyon. The Great Barrier Reef. Niagara

Falls. Snow-capped mountains. Lush, green rain forests. Rolling hills. An indescribable sunset. Double rainbows. If Jarod were the only human being on this entire planet, I would not have shorted him at all. I would have given as much attention to detail—rhyme and color and the variety of species—just for him.

Wow.

Don't ever forget, My child, that I love him that much.

That's incredible, God!

And I love *you* that much too.

It doesn't feel like it.

Disobedience—

I know. I know. Disobedience will do that.

Right.

So it's not about Jarod?

Well, partly. But it's also about you. Each person must take responsibility for his or her own actions.

Yeah, I guess.

So . . . are you ready to talk?

Sigh. All right.

Go ahead.

I love him.

I'm listening.

And he loves me.

And?

So we love each other.

Go on.

Well, that's it.

No, it's not.

Well, how far are we going with this?

Let's talk about how far *you're* going.

I knew this was coming.

What do you want to tell Me?

I don't *want* to tell You anything. But since I *need* to . . . and since You already know . . . well, okay. Here it is: We're not having sex.
Go on.
That's enough, isn't it?
No. We need to talk it out.
This is really personal, God. I mean . . . this is intimate stuff.
My child. I *created* You. You can't get more intimate than that.
Well, yeah. But still . . . Jarod and I aren't having sex.
What are you having?
A good time. But it's not sex.
What *is* sex?
Well, You know. You created it, remember?
Yes, but I want to hear it from you.
Sex . . . is . . . well, it's . . . intercourse.
Intercourse.
Yeah. Intercourse.
That's it?
Intercourse. Sex is two people having intercourse.
Hm. I'd say it's a lot more than that.
Whaddya mean? How can sex be more than intercourse?
Sex is the uniting of two people in an intimate way.
Through intercourse.
It's two bodies intertwining together—physically, emotionally, spiritually. Again, sex is way more than intercourse. You said it yourself: I invented sex.
Yeah?
So since I invented it, I ought to have a say in how and where it works best. And that's in marriage. My plan is for you to remain sexually pure until marriage.
But, I am! I'm not having sex.
Correction: You're not having *intercourse*. But you are *not* living a sexually pure lifestyle.

How come? I'm a virgin!

You can technically be a virgin without being sexually pure.

What?

Thousands of young adults walk down a church aisle to be joined in marriage proclaiming their virginity. But guess what?

What?

I'm not as interested in your virginity as I am in your sexual purity.

But—

Anyone can say no to intercourse.

And I have!

But it takes a lot more than simply refraining from intercourse to be sexually pure.

So what are we talking about?

We're talking about you and Jarod.

We love each other.

You and Jarod have become one.

But how? We've never done it.

You've never had intercourse, but you *have* become intimately acquainted with each other's bodies.

But we never—

You've been intimate.

No. We really haven't. . . .

Dishonesty. Disobedience. Remember the reasons you've felt so distant from Me?

Well, yeah. But, God, we never . . . I mean, we . . . uh . . .

It's just us. Come on. Be specific.

I don't. He never. I mean, I um—

You can be intimate with him yet have trouble just *talking* about it with Me?

No. Well, yeah. Hey, this is embarrassing.

Okay. I'll start. Again . . . you've been intimate with each other. Your hands have gone where they shouldn't. You've crossed boundaries that should be reserved only for marriage.

But we never had sex!

Yes, you did. Sex is intimacy with someone of the opposite sex. You and Jarod have been intimate.

I . . . I . . .

Even though you've never had intercourse, you are NOT sexually pure.

Well then I might as well have intercourse!

In My mind, you already have.

What?!?

Have you been intimate with Jarod?

Yes.

Did it ever cross your mind that this is what you'd like to be doing with your future husband?

Well, yeah.

You've allowed Jarod to experience something with you that should be shared only with your future husband.

But—

And in a sense, you've stolen from Jarod's future wife.

I don't get it.

You're giving him an intimacy that only she should experience with Jarod.

Well . . . why didn't You stop me?

I'll never treat you like a puppet. You'll always have free will. I'll never force you to obey My commands. But I *did* use My Holy Spirit to prick your conscience.

Is that why I was feeling guilty?

Yes.

And that's why I was feeling so far away from You?

Yes. Again . . . disobedience will do that.

But, God . . . we love each other.

Do you love *Me?*

Sure.

Pick it up.

What?

Your Student Bible.

Yeah, here it is.

Flip over to John 14:21. What's it say?

It's pretty much saying that if I love You, I'll obey You. So, what are You saying? That I don't love You?

No, *you're* saying it . . . by your actions.

But God, I love You. Come on!

If you really love Me, you'll obey Me. You'll want to please Me. You'll allow *Me* to guide you . . . instead of Jarod . . . or your emotions.

Are You saying I've sinned?

That's exactly what I'm saying.

Well, in Your eyes, if I've already had sex, I might as well actually go ahead and do it!

Oh no, My child. There are always consequences.

What hope do I have?

You have all kinds of hope. I *am* hope!

I don't get it.

Forgiveness. It's yours for the asking.

Well, sure, for stuff like lying and cheating and saying bad words or watching a movie I shouldn't have seen. But sex?

Yes.

You'll forgive me for going too far physically?

Yes. If you *seek* forgiveness.

Okay. Will You forgive me?

Not yet.

What?!? You just said—

Repentance, My child. It's all about repentance.

But I *did* repent. I just asked You to forg—

True repentance means "I don't ever plan on going down that road

again," NOT "I'll get forgiven now, and after Jarod and I make out tomorrow night, I'll get forgiven again."

Hey, how'd You know I was thinking that?

Who are you talking to?

God. Right.

Repentance reflects the condition of your heart.

Well, my heart wants to be forgiven.

Not really.

Come on, God!

You're still not convinced you've actually sinned. You're sorry . . . but mainly sorry you're being called on it. You're sorry you've been "caught." You're sorry you've felt so distanced from Me. And you're sorry you haven't been praying or reading your Bible. But . . . you're not *really* sorry you've been intimate with Jarod.

Father, we love each other.

Do you want a lifetime of sexual fulfillment . . . or a night here and there of short-lived experiences?

Definitely a lifetime!

Do you want a partner . . . or a soul mate—a man who's as crazy about you when you reek with bad breath and wake with a bed-head as he is when you're wearing that little red dress with the red shoes?

Wow. Bed-head. No makeup.

And when you're sick . . . head over the toilet battling the flu.

And stinky.

That, My child, is a soul mate. *That* is true love.

I don't have that with Jarod.

No, you don't.

How come?

A couple of reasons: Jarod is basing your relationship on feelings, not commitment. You see, commitment is a *decision*. It overrides feelings.

I'm not sure I know what You mean.

If the commitment is there, what you look like—how much weight you gain through the years, a terminal illness you may suffer, the disfigurement you may receive from an auto accident—will not decrease the love factor between the two of you . . . because your love will be based on commitment, not feelings.

I guess feelings can be pretty fleeting, huh?

Exactly. Here today, gone tomorrow.

Wow. What Jarod and I have is special . . . but it's nowhere near *that* deep!

Let me ask you something.

K.

Ever heard of alopecia areata?

No.

It's a disease that affects thousands.

What is it?

It's an autoimmune deficiency. Your immune system thinks you're allergic to your own hair. So, basically . . . you start losing your hair.

You mean . . . go bald?

Right.

Is it men or women or both?

Both, but mostly women.

Old women?

No. Mostly young women—even children and teenagers.

Wow. I can't imagine.

Here's the question: If you contracted alopecia, would your relationship with Jarod change at all?

Are You kidding? Jarod *loves* my hair. He's always playing with it, smelling it, . . . well . . .

But why would your relationship change?

Well . . . because. I mean, I'd be lacking something. I wouldn't be all there. I mean . . . I *want* to say it wouldn't matter—it wouldn't matter at all. But—somehow deep inside—I'd be kidding myself. I *know* it would matter to him. Things would change.

How would your relationship change?

Well, it probably wouldn't take long for Jarod to find another healthy head of hair. I think he'd stick with me at the beginning—You know, try to comfort me and all that. But . . .

But six or seven months later?

I don't like admitting this . . . but I really believe he'd move on.

Hm. What if you had to have a mastectomy?

At *my* age?

It would be extremely rare, but it *could* happen.

Oh, please, God. Don't even go there.

Think about it.

Okay, but only for a second.

Fair enough. Would this change in your outer appearance affect your relationship with Jarod?

Yeah, probably . . . eventually.

My child, these are real possibilities that can happen in a lifetime. But over the course of years, a marriage built on Me can withstand *any* obstacle.

Wow. I've never known a love like that.

I love you like that.

Yes, but You're GOD. I've never known human love like that.

That's because you've never been in an opposite-sex relationship that has been centered on Me.

Oh.

Which brings Me to the second reason.

Huh?

Remember, a few minutes ago? We were talking about being a soul mate with your future husband. You said that you and Jarod have never had that.

Oh, yeah. And I asked why.

And I said . . .

A couple of reasons. One is because our relationship is based on feelings instead of commitment—real commitment that can weather the storms of life changes and disease and everyday struggles.

Right.

And the second reason?

Your relationship is not centered on Me.

So, can we *get* it centered on You?

You've just told me that Jarod isn't your soul mate—that he probably *wouldn't* stay through the long haul if things became difficult. Why would you want to continue a relationship that's surface . . . temporary?

Because he's all I have!

Hm.

Oh, wow. Did I actually say that out loud?

Yes.

Oooh.

But even if you hadn't, I still would have heard your thoughts.

Oh, yeah.

My child, I long for you to trust *Me* with your love life.

But, God, I want someone who's—

Capable of making you feel secure? And cherished? A young man who's not afraid to cry with you? Someone who will spontaneously surprise you with a picnic lunch by the lake? Fly a kite with you on a windy day? Romance you? Bring you flowers? Someone who's strong. Deeply committed to Me. Involved in church. One who helps Widow Foster out of her car and up the steps to church on Sunday morning. A young man who stops in the hallway between Sunday school and morning worship to pick up a three-year-old and tousle his hair. Someone who makes you laugh and who treats you like a princess. Someone who's head-over-heels crazy about you and really doesn't care if your hair is long or short or if you had the extra helping of dessert you really

didn't need. A man who's excited about providing for you. One who brings out the very best in you and enhances your relationship with Me.

I don't know what to say.

That's whom you're longing for . . . isn't it?

Oh, yes, Father. That's the cry of my heart! That's *exactly* the man I want to spend the rest of my life with!

Is Jarod that man?

You know he isn't.

Go on.

Jesus, he's nowhere near that description.

Then why are you dating him?

I . . . I . . . I *thought* we loved each other. But now . . . after all this . . . oooh. I hate admitting this, but I think I've been dating him . . . just to date him. You know. It felt good. I belonged to someone. And I like the attention. It feels good to be kissed and . . . well, You know.

Do you believe now that I know exactly the kind of man you want . . . you need?

Oh, yes! You hit the nail right on the head! You gave a *perfect* description of the man I want to marry.

Then trust Me.

I trust You.

Trust Me with your love life.

Oh, that.

Trust that in My perfect timing, *I* will bring exactly whom I want in your life.

But that may take a while! I know Your timing, God. You're just not as fast as I wish You were.

But I'm never late.

But You *do* take a while.

Will you trust Me?

Well . . . what if You forget me and—

There's only one thing I forget.

What's that?

Forgiven sins.

Smile.

Everything else is right at the forefront of My mind.

But . . . You're dealing with persecuted Christians in Sudan, and earthquakes in Turkey, and high-school shootings, and drug busts, and—

And your future.

You mean . . .

Your friends and your relationships are every bit as important to Me as disease and famine and all the other wrongs in the world.

No way.

Believe it. Everything that concerns you, concerns Me.

That's incredible. I don't deserve that kind of attention.

I watched my Son die so you *could* have this kind of attention.

I'm so sorry, Father.

It's starting.

What?

Your heart is beginning to look like a repentant heart.

I think I'm finally beginning to understand.

I'm listening.

I don't want to steal from my future husband.

No.

I've been selfish. I've been with Jarod for what *I* could get out of the relationship. I mean, he made me feel special. He was someone to take me to Homecoming and to go out with on weekends. And . . . well, the physical stuff . . . it felt good.

That's because I created you as a sexual being. It's *supposed* to feel good—but it's also supposed to be *saved* for one man.

The man you described?

Yes. The man who is My choice for your lifetime mate.

I feel sick at my stomach.

Oh?

Yeah. I'm so sorry I became involved with Jarod, Father. It all seems so stupid now! I mean . . . he's not the man You described. And if I know he's not the man I want and need in a soul mate, why am I messing around with him? You're right, God. I've cheated him. I have given him physically and emotionally what only his wife should.

Even though you didn't have intercourse?

Yeah. I see it now, God. Even though we didn't have intercourse, we were still bonded together. We felt as one—emotionally, physically. Oh . . . I am so sorry! I mean, I really am, God. I am really, really sorry! I can't believe I rationalized all that. I actually talked myself into believing everything was fine—that what we were doing was permissible because we loved each other. But if real love is the way You described it—something that overrides feelings—Jarod and I are nowhere near that. We don't have real love, God. What we have . . . is . . . well . . . what *do* we have?

Lust.

Ouch.

You have a relationship based on physical attraction.

You make it sound so surface. And it *is* . . . I just . . . Man! I'm ashamed, Father. I'm really sorry. This is not what I want. Not at all.

***Now* you're ready.**

Ready? For what?

To seek forgiveness. You have a repentant heart.

Oh, God, I really do seek Your forgiveness. I don't *ever* plan to go down this road again. I want to save myself for my future husband. Will You forgive me, Father?

I forgive you.

And will You help me?

Yes. I forgive . . . and I forget. And I would *love* to help you, but I need you to do your part.

Anything, Father. What is it?

I need you to give Me total control of your love life.

And that means . . .

Let Me write your love story. Trust Me to bring the right man into your life. I want to relieve you of all that pressure.

But I still have to be on the lookout, right?

No. You don't have to do anything except be totally in love with Me.

You mean . . . I don't even have to *look* for him?

No. That's My job. *Your* job is to trust Me. Remember, I know you better than you even know yourself, because I created you. I know—even more than you do—what and who will fulfill you, make you happy, draw you continually closer to Me. I know all that. Trust Me with it.

This sounds too good to be true.

Believe it.

I don't even have to *look* for him?

All you have to do . . . is be totally in love with Me.

How do I get more in love with You, Father?

How do you become more acquainted with *anyone?*

Hm. I spend time with him. Tell him stuff. Listen to him. We do things together.

Works the same way with Me.

Sounds easy.

Spend time with Me—the way you used to. Remember when you were looking for your CD and found your Student Bible?

Yeah.

You were reminiscing about camp days and how close we were. There was a time you couldn't wait to tell Me everything. A time you longed to open My Word and read and grow.

Yeah! I want that again. I really want that again, Father.

I'm still in the same place. You're the one who moved, remember?

Yeah. I'm so sorry. God, now that You've forgiven me, let's start over, okay? I'd really love to have a clean slate.

It's yours.

But I'm gonna need help.

That's what I'm here for.

I mean . . . right now it's all so clear. But I'm afraid when Jarod looks at me with those puppy-dog eyes, I'm gonna melt right into his hands.

I can give you the strength to call it off with Jarod.

I need to do that, don't I?

Yes. We've already established the fact that he's not the man I want you to spend the rest of your life with.

It's still going to be hard.

Yes, but you're not alone. And after you've ended your relationship with Jarod, I want to teach you about healthy, godly boundaries. I want to teach you how to live a sexually pure lifestyle.

Doesn't that just mean not going too far with the opposite sex?

No, it's a lot more than that. Sexual purity is a *lifestyle*.

What do You mean, God?

It involves what you listen to and watch, how you act and react. It's establishing holy safeguards around your life—protecting yourself from the deceit of Satan.

Yeah, I'll need You to help me big-time with all that. We've got a lot of work to do, huh, Father?

And one more thing.

Yeah?

Trusting Me with your love life . . . means trusting Me *forever* with your love life.

I *think* I know what You mean.

Let's make sure.

Okay.

Remember . . . I want to establish a love life with you. I want you

to be so in love with Me that your biggest concern is simply growing closer to Me.

I want that too, God. And I'm going to spend time with You and continue to give You all of me, so we *can* have that kind of relationship.

What if I choose not to bring a man into your life?

What?

What if I choose not to share you with a man?

Oh, God. You would do that?

My ways are not for you to know yet.

Oh, Father, You know my heart. You know my desires.

Yes, I created you.

I never thought that You might choose to keep me single.

What if I do?

A lifetime of being alone?

Not alone. My child. You are never alone.

I know.

What if I choose not to share you with a man?

I can't understand that, God.

I know. But with My strength, you can *accept without understanding*.

Accept without understanding.

That's spiritual maturity.

In Your strength, I can accept without understanding.

In My strength . . . you can accept without understanding.

Wow.

Do you trust Me?

Yes, God. I do.

Do you love Me?

Yes, Father. And I want to love You more.

Yes?

Yes! I want to fall in love with You more and more every single day of my life.

Yes!

God, You know my heart. You created me. You know I yearn for a husband—the man You described earlier. I'm trusting You for him. But if . . . for reasons I'll never understand . . . You choose *not* to bring him into my life, I'm still going to trust You. It will *not* affect my relationship with You.

Yes!

I love You, God. I really, really love You. *You*, Father, are the love of my life. And until You bring Your choice for a lifetime mate—or even if You don't—I'm simply going to concentrate on being in love with You.

I'm so proud of you, My child. I love you more than you'll ever comprehend.

But, God?

Yes?

What about my physical involvement with Jarod? I wish I'd never gone down that path.

Me too . . . but you're forgiven. In fact, I've already wiped your slate clean. It's forgotten.

I commit my sexual purity to You, God.

Thank you. I'll give you the strength to *keep* that commitment.

I need to break if off with Jarod.

I'll go with you.

Thanks. I'll need all the help I can get.

I'll give you the words. I'll provide the strength.

I love You, God! I love You!

And I love *you*, My child.

Hm. So if I'm committed to being sexually pure, does that mean kissing is a sin?

Let me just share my heart, okay? I don't believe it's wrong to kiss someone you care deeply about and are in a relationship with. But simply kissing someone is a far cry from making out. I define "making out" as prolonged and deep kissing with petting (touching each other's private parts), and this should clearly be reserved for marriage and marriage only!

I also believe that way too many teen girls give their kisses away too freely. Think about it: Every time you kiss someone, you're giving a piece of yourself away. Does that make it wrong? No. But it *does* make your kisses extremely valuable. So be incredibly selective about whom you choose to kiss. Let God help you with that decision. He cares about your kisses!

Kissing someone just because it feels good . . . or kissing someone simply to be kissing someone . . . are not good enough reasons to be kissing! The key is to have no regrets. If Christ is truly LORD of every area of your life (including your dates), you'll be careful to follow His leading.

I'm still single, but I've been in some wonderful dating relationships. The key is, I have no regrets. I've chosen to date only godly men, and I've never gone past a kiss. I'm thankful for the relationships I've had, and I've been careful to keep Christ in charge of each one.

Give your kisses . . . as well as your future dates to God. Ask Him to help you live a life of no regrets.

14

On Missions

I said: God, I really need help with this research project.

He said: Well, you're in the right spot. No place like the library.

Hey! There's the church bulletin from yesterday's service. I forgot I had stuffed that in my backpack with my Bible.

Good service, wasn't it?

Yeah. That missionary speaker was great!

Did you agree with what he said?

You bet! We can never do too much to evangelize the world.

I noticed you gave $20 for the missions offering.

Oh, yeah! I'm all *for* missions. There's nothing more important than leading people to You, Lord.

Really?

Well, sure!

Hm. What about Olivia?

Olivia Wilson?

Uh-huh.

Well . . . what about her?

She doesn't know Me.

That's an understatement. She's one of the wildest girls in my school.

Know *why* she's wild?

Cuz she's a sinner!

Because she's empty and hurting inside. She's looking in all the wrong places for fulfillment and love and meaning.

Yeah. That's too bad.

So what are you going to do about it?

Huh?

What are you going to do about it?

What do You mean?

You just said there's nothing more important than bringing people to Me.

Well, yeah . . . but I'm talking about *missions*, God.

This is missions.

You know—Africa.

Olivia is missions.

Olivia's a basket case. A lost cause. She's hopeless.

You would be too, without Me.

Okay. Okay. I get it. If You really want me to talk to Olivia, I'll do it. But I won't know what to say!

That's all right. You're covered.

Whaddya mean?

You've got your Bible open. Flip back a few pages to Jeremiah.

Okay. Jeremiah.

Read Jeremiah 1:6-9.

Here goes: "'O Lord God,' I said, 'I can't do that! I'm far too young! I'm only a youth.'

" 'Don't say that,' he replied, 'for you will go wherever I send you and speak whatever I tell you to. And don't be afraid of the people, for I, the Lord, will be with you and see you through.'

"Then he touched my mouth and said, 'See, I have put my words in your mouth!' " (TLB).

You don't have to worry about what to say. That's My responsibility.

My responsibility is simply being willing, right?

Right.

And if she makes fun of me or rejects me?

Just as I told Jeremiah: "Don't be afraid of the people. I will be with you and see you through."

I think I'll start out by inviting her to the concert our youth group is going to. I could even buy her ticket.

Now you're talking. I appreciate your willingness to follow My lead. And I love your tender heart.

Thanks, Lord.

But there's something else we need to talk about.

What's that?

The $20 you placed in the missions offering.

Should I have given more?

It's not the amount I want to talk with you about.

Then what is it?

The reason you gave.

Well, I gave . . . because, You know. It's missions!

And?

I wanna do my part.

What *is* your part?

You know—supporting it.

Supporting what?

Supporting missions. Supporting the cause of evangelism—bringing the lost to You.

It's not really a cause, you know.

Well, what would You call it?

I'd say it's more of a command.

That's pretty strong!

Yes, it is. Check out Mark 16:15.

Okay. "Go into all the world and preach the good news to all creation."

Does that sound like a suggestion or a command?

A command.

So what are you going to do about it?

I'm going to support it, God! That's why I gave $20. And I'll give more if You want me to. I don't really have it right now, but I'll get some extra baby-sitting jobs, and maybe a part-time job at the burger stand, and—

I'm not asking you for more money right now.

I don't get it. What *are* You asking of me, Father?

I'm asking you to catch My vision.

I don't get it.

My vision is that the entire world will hear My good news of salvation.

Yes! And I support that.

You support that . . . in Africa . . . with $20.

Well, yeah.

I want more.

I said I'd give more—

More of *you*.

More of me?

Missions isn't simply placing money in the offering plate, relieved that someone else is obeying the command to spread the gospel. Missions is obeying that command yourself. *Missions is living out that command!*

But how can I do that, God? I'm only a junior in high school. I can't go to Africa.

I didn't ask you to go to Africa. I may ask you later, but I'm not asking you now.

So what *are* You asking me, Father?

I've placed you in a mission field. I'm asking you to obey the command to spread the gospel in your own mission field.

You've placed *me* in a mission field?

That's right.

But God, I'm in Omaha, Nebraska!

Right. And you're enrolled in *what* school?

Central High.

And you work *where*?

Taco Tim's.

And you play soccer *with whom*?

The junior-varsity squad.

And you work out *where*?

At the fitness center downtown. You mean—

That's right. My child.

My school, my athletics, my job, what I do in my spare time—it's my mission field, isn't it?

It sure is!

Wow! I never thought of that before.

And it's a field ripe for harvest.

I always thought missions was something overseas. You know, something that cost a lot of money. Something you could only do full time after college.

I'd love for you to start right now.

I'm a missionary!

You're a missionary.

Just like Jeremiah?

And Daniel. And Shadrach. And Esther. And Paul. And anyone else who's taken a stand for Me and spread My Word.

What an honor!

Are you ready?

I can't do this on my own, You know.

You won't have to. None of my missionaries are on their own.

I'm scared . . . but I'm willing.

I love your tenderness!

Where do we start?

Right there.

Where?

Two tables over—in the reference section of this library.

Hey! It's Olivia!

❋ And I've already begun softening her heart.

Okay, I'm going, Lord.

No. *We're* going.

Right. *We're* going!

Myth: Missions only happen overseas.

Fact: Missions happen every time you share the gospel with a nonbeliever.

Mission trips are so popular, it's easy to believe that evangelism isn't real unless you've paid big bucks to participate on a mission trip in a Third-World country. If you're canoeing down the Amazon River, fighting off crocodiles to carry the *Jesus* film to an unreached people group, you're truly involved in missions.

Hey, the truth is . . . you don't even have to leave your hometown to be a missionary! God can just as easily use you to serve at your local soup kitchen or to reach out to the kid at your school who's in detention more than he's in science class as He can use you in a small, African village.

The important thing isn't where you serve, it's simply that you serve. Christ calls us to be servants. The people around you will know you're a Christian because of your love and your servant's heart—and that can be evidenced anywhere! But if God *does* lead you into an overseas missions experience, don't assume that's more important than what He's choosing to do through your Christian friends who stay home. Both areas of service are necessary and equally as important.

People all over the world (including those in your geometry class) need God, because they're confused as to what real truth is. We're living in a post-modern society that screams, "There IS no absolute truth." But when you have an active, intimate, growing relationship with Truth Itself, you want to lead others into that knowledge, into that relationship.

As you head into the next conversation, ask God to bring specific people to your mind who are confused about absolute truth—people who are being deceived by false doctrines and beliefs. And ask Him to give you opportunities to be a missionary to those friends.

15

On Absolute Truth

God said: Abbie's really confused.

I said: It's no big deal.

Yes, it is a big deal. She's searching . . . and she's looking in the wrong direction.

So she's looking at different religions. She has doubts.

And it's what she's doing with those doubts that concerns Me.

I don't get it.

Christianity can take doubt, My child. Christianity can take every doubt the world cares to toss My way, or it wouldn't have lasted more than two thousand years. But it's when people refuse to *give* Me their doubts that it becomes wrong.

You mean, You want us to tell You what we doubt about Christianity?

That's right. How else can I replace those doubts with solid faith?

It's when you harbor the doubt—stuff it inside and refuse to allow Me to walk you through it—that it becomes detrimental.

Okay, then. Here goes. I can identify with Abbie.

Go on.

Well . . . I'm having doubts. Abbie's talking about other religions and reincarnation and stuff. I don't know; it sounds interesting.

My child, reincarnation is simply wishful thinking for those whose lives aren't right with Me. If you want the truth, check out Hebrews 9:27.

Yeah, I guess I could do that. Here it is: "Just as man is destined to die once, and after that to face judgment."

How much room does that Scripture leave for the possibility of reincarnation?

None.

That's right. Reincarnation is a lie from Satan.

But . . . as long as it's okay to give You my doubts . . . can we keep talking for a while?

Sure. I *love* talking with you, My child.

Even when I'm not full of praise and all that kind of stuff?

An honest heart is what I'm after. Give Me your honesty.

Okay, here goes. I'm not sure about Christianity, God. I mean . . . how could only one religion be right? Shouldn't everyone just believe what's right for him or her?

To a serial killer, it's right for him to kill. Does that mean it's right in My eyes?

Well, no. But now You're talking about killing. I'm just talking about religious beliefs.

What you're *really* talking about is truth.

Yeah! What's right and wrong is going to differ from person to person. *I* should get to decide what's right for me!

But simply because you *decide* something, doesn't make it so.

It should! If I decide it's right for me to drive when I'm fourteen instead of sixteen, it should be okay.

No. Your thoughts and decisions can't change reality.

Huh?

The laws of your land are a reality that state you can't drive until
you're sixteen.

But if I *decide*—

Okay, let's say you *decide* you're the wealthiest person in the world.
Guess what—you're really not. You can *decide* that all you want, but
reality says that's not the truth.

Oooh. You got me there.

You see, My child . . . there *has* to be an absolute truth—a standard
of right and wrong—by which everyone can measure their lives.

But what if I believe that—

Stop. Listen to yourself. There must be something deeper than your
beliefs. There has to be something that goes way beyond your
futile thinking, something much higher on which you can base
your standards and your lifestyle.

Why can't I decide that for myself?

Because if everyone decided that for themselves, life would be
utter chaos. Dylan Klebold and Eric Harris decided it was "right" for
them to murder innocent students at Columbine High School. But
simply because that's what they decided didn't make it right. *You*
can't determine the standard for right. It's above and beyond you.

Okay, but let's get back to religion. There must be lots of different
truths out there since there are so many religions.

No, My child. There's one Truth.

Then why all the different religions?

Because people want to distort reality.

I don't get it.

They want to rationalize the wrong they're doing and feel good
about it. If you search hard enough, you can find a religion to support just about anything.

So . . . I could find a religion that would tell me it's okay to smoke pot?

You could. And you could find a religion that condones sex outside of marriage—as long as you love the person you're involved with.

Wow! So what's the problem?

The problem is reality. Remember, you can believe what you want . . . but that doesn't make it true. You can believe that someday man will evolve into rattlesnakes and you can start a church that supports that belief, but that doesn't make it reality. Man will never become a rattlesnake! But you can believe it.

Why would I want to believe something that's not true?

Hm. Good question. So why are you looking at other religions?

Well . . . how do I know they're not true? I mean, of course Christianity is true for *You*, because You're God. But what if it's not true for me?

Relativism.

What-if-ism?

Relativism. It's the view that there's not one absolute truth. Everything is relative. Just because something's wrong for Abbie doesn't necessarily mean it's wrong for you.

Yeah! That's what I believe! Relativism. I like that!

Doesn't hold water.

What?!?

You can't create truth simply by believing it.

Oh, man! Why do we keep coming back to this?

Because your search for absolute truth is what's lying beneath all this stuff.

But I gotta know. I really wanna know about other religions. How can I know for sure that Christianity is the right one—that Christianity is the *real* truth?

There is absolutely nothing we can't talk about. So let's do it.

Okay. What about Hinduism? That sounds pretty good.

If you believe Jesus Christ was simply a good person teaching spiritual things, you'll be attracted to Hinduism. Believers can choose which gods they want to worship, but no one has a personal relationship with *any* god.

Hm. I'd miss the personal relationship part. Is reincarnation part of this religion?

Yes, and the way Hindus escape the cycle of reincarnation is by following the right religious disciplines.

So if I mess up and *don't* follow the right disciplines, I'm history?

That's right.

Hm. Okay, Hinduism isn't for me. I believe that Your Son was much more than just a good teacher. What about Buddhism?

Buddhists don't believe in Me. They'll tell you there *is* no God. They'll also tell you that you can become godlike through spiritual enlightenment.

Enlightenment?

They'll tell you that to achieve true happiness, you must separate yourself from material things.

Whoa! I'm not ready to give up my Gameboy, or our family's big-screen TV, or my roller blades, or—

They don't believe My Son Jesus was the Messiah, and a good Buddhist is someone who helps others and loves everyone.

But for what? What's the point?

Exactly.

Abbie says Islam is looking good.

Abbie's confused, remember? Muslims don't believe Jesus was God. They think My Son was simply a prophet.

So who *is* God?

Muslims say that Allah is God, and they'll tell you that you can only be saved through Allah by praying five times a day, making a trip to Mecca, making financial contributions, fasting, and confessing your faith.

That's ridiculous! That's saying we can earn our salvation. What if I don't wanna go to Mecca?

Then you'd never make it in Islam.

Well, Judaism believes that God is God. Jews believe You are Who You say You are, right?

Yes and no.

Whaddya mean?

Judaism says that I am God, and I am God alone.

That sounds right.

But it's *not* right. Jews don't believe that My Son Jesus and My Holy Spirit are part of Me. They'll tell you there's no such thing as the Trinity (Myself, My Son, Jesus, and My Holy Spirit all being one).

Well, what *do* they believe?

They're hoping that someday I will send a messiah to save the Jewish people.

But I thought You already sent the Messiah. I thought Jesus was the Messiah.

He was. And He still is.

I guess they're confused, huh?

Yes. So is Abbie. And so are you.

I don't *want* to be confused, Father. I really *wanna* get it right.

Okay. Then let's keep talking. You can choose to believe a man-made religion, and you can deceive yourself into thinking you can create your own truth—which, remember, means you also have to create your own reality—or you can simply choose to accept Christianity and know that I really am absolute Truth.

Well, I *do* believe that Jesus Christ is Your Son, Father. And I *do* believe that You and Jesus and the Holy Spirit are all a part of each other. I don't understand it all, but I believe it.

So what's the problem?

Well . . . I don't know. I guess I just get all confused when my friends at school start talking about truth and what's right. I mean, when Katie says, "Just because it's true for you doesn't mean it's true for me." And when Abbie starts talking about reincarnation and coming back as the queen of some far-off country and that she has the right to believe whatever she wants . . . I don't know; I just get all confused and don't know what to say.

My child, you don't have to know what to say. Your lifestyle will always speak louder than your words.

But . . . still . . . I—

Katie and Abbie are going to search for a while. But as they're searching, be an example for them in your life and your actions.

Hey! That sounds familiar!

You memorized it back when you were in middle school.

Oh, yeah! It's 1 Timothy 4:12.

Want to say it again?

Sure! I love that verse: "Don't let anyone look down on you because you are young, but set an example for the believers in speech, in life, in love, in faith, and in purity."

Let them see the difference between Christianity and all other religions through how you live your life!

But what do I say when they ask me questions?

Remember, you don't have to know all the answers. But you *should* know what you believe and why you believe it. Let's go through the basics, okay?

Okay. Christianity states that everyone is born with sin.

Right. But you have a choice.

Yeah. I can choose to keep living in sin, or I can ask You to forgive me and I can start living in obedience to You.

And how do you earn this forgiveness?

I can't earn it.

Right!

But I can get it by trusting You to save me and forgive me and believing that You died for me.

And was death the final act?

No way. You conquered death and sent Your Holy Spirit to live inside me to guide me and to empower me to live a godly life.

Yes!

It's so cool that Christianity offers eternal life for *free!*

It's because I love you.

Thank You so much, Father.

So are we clear on absolute truth?

Hm. Let's see. I think You've written something about that, haven't You?

Smile.

Ah. Here it is: "I am the way and the truth and the life. No one comes to the Father except through me" (John 14:6). That was Jesus talking. It was You speaking through Him, wasn't it?

Yes, My child.

Father, I love it that we can talk about anything.

Anything and everything.

Everything?

You name it.

It's that Mrs. Johnson. She gives us *waaay* too much history homework.

Smile.

16

On Getting Married

I said: Wasn't Julie's wedding gorgeous?

God said: Yes, it was.

God, I want that.

I know you do.

No, I mean . . . I *yearn* for that.

I know. I created you, remember?

But I don't even have a boyfriend! And here I am always dreaming about my wedding and being married and having a family. I want a perfect man.

I can't give you a perfect man—but I *can* give you a perfect husband.

Really? Are You kidding? Talk to me!

I want to be your Husband.

Oh.

You act surprised.

Well . . . it's just that I was thinking of . . . You know, someone I could put my arms around.

Yes, I understand your desire for a human spouse, but the fact that I want to be your Husband shouldn't come as a surprise to you. I've already proposed.

You have?

Yes. I sent My only Son to invite you to the wedding.

He paid a high price.

Yes, He did.

I never thought of it this way before.

And I've sent you the invitation . . . more than once.

You have?

Yes. Read it. You'll find it in Jeremiah 3:14.

Jeremiah? Okay, that's right after Isaiah. Here it is: "For I am your husband." Wow. I've never read that!

And you can read the invitation again in Isaiah 54:5.

Got it right here: "For your Maker is your husband—the LORD Almighty is his name." Oh, my goodness! You're not kidding!

No, I'm not. Sending My only Son to give His life was certainly no joke.

I feel so . . . I don't know . . . embarrassed that I'd never gotten that before.

You're human; therefore, it's natural to dream of your human spouse. That's how I created you. And I desire that for you . . . someday. But I can help prepare you for your future family right now.

How?

By helping you fall in love with Me.

I don't get it.

In order for you to truly experience a fulfilling, wonderful marriage with a Christian man, you first have to be totally grounded and whole in Me.

Keep talking.

I want to be your first and foremost Husband. You are My bride.

Yes! I've read that in the Bible . . . that the Church is the Bride of Christ.

Yes, but I don't want you to think in general terms such as "the Church." I want to personalize it. I want to give you the greatest wedding imaginable. I want you to make a deep, sacred, eternal covenant with Me.

So, we're not really talking about a ceremony, are we God?

We can have a ceremony. But before we do, I want to make sure you understand what an eternal covenant with Me is all about.

Well, I assume You mean being a Christian. I've been a Christian for five years.

Yes, you have. Five years ago, you asked Me to forgive your sins and be a part of your life. But let's take it to a deeper level.

I'm not following You, Lord.

A husband and wife become engaged; then they get married.

Right.

When you asked Me to come into your life and forgive your sins, we became engaged.

Yeah.

And the engagement process is a tremendous learning experience.

I've gotta admit, I've sure learned a lot in the last five years!

Yes, you have. You've grown spiritually through Bible studies and through your church—

And through the Christian club I'm in.

Yes. I'm excited about your spiritual growth. But no one can remain engaged forever.

Yeah, I know that's true with humans, but how does that apply to a spiritual marriage with You, Father?

I want you to become one with Me.

Now I'm totally lost!

That's what holiness is all about, My child—becoming one with your heavenly Father. And that's what marriage is all about. I'm asking you to become one with Me, spiritually.

What does that mean?

It means that someday, if I choose to wed you with another man, he will always take second place to Me. I have to be your first marriage in order for your earthly marriage—your second marriage—to be as good as I want it to be.

Okay. I'm beginning to see what You're saying. This is totally new to me. I mean, I've never thought of my relationship with You in terms of a spiritual marriage, but I like it. So what's my next step?

To become one with Me—to establish and maintain an eternal covenant with Me—I need total commitment.

But I'm already committed to You, Father.

I'm talking about something much deeper than knowing I forgive your sins. It's not about simply accepting the fact that I've forgiven you. I want to be *inside* you. I want to flow through your veins and burn in your bones.

Wow. We *are* talking deep, aren't we?

Listen, My child. I want to affect the way you act and react. I want the things that make *Me* cry to bring tears to *your* eyes.

But . . . I don't know You that well, Father.

Exactly.

No, I didn't mean—

You're exactly right. To know what breaks My heart, You have to *have* My heart. You've got to feel My very heart beat. Know My passion. Recognize the putrid scent of sin that I smell. Hear the weeping of broken hearts. Learn the sight of hopelessness. Be able to touch broken dreams.

Wow. I'm nowhere near that, God. But I sure would like to be.

To know Me on that intimate level requires becoming one with Me. This isn't a flippant promise we're talking about!

No! It's a sacred oath I'm asking you to make, an eternal covenant.

What will this require? I mean . . . how do I give You everything I am?

Not only everything you are, but everything you ever hope to become.

Yes, God. My heart yearns for that. I *want* that deep, intimate relationship with You.

Well, for the past five years, you've expected Me to follow you around.

I thought that's what the Bible said You'd do!

Yes, the Bible says I'll never leave you.

Right.

But My role is not that of a puppy.

I'm lost here, God.

It's not my job to follow you around as if I'm holding a magic wand blessing this and blessing that.

Then how's it *supposed* to be?

My child, I'm already at work! You're merely a part in My giant kaleidoscope of spectacular plans.

I like that!

But recognize you're a *part* of My eternal plan. You're not the plan itself.

Okay.

Therefore, your responsibility is to see where I'm at work and to join with Me and become a part of all I'm doing.

Oh, my goodness! I'm starting to get it now, Lord! I've had it all backwards. You're right. I thought You were all too happy just to be a part of my life. But that's not the way it should be at all. *I* should be a part of *Your* life—and all that You're doing!

Right. When you enter an eternal covenant with Me, you're not only giving Me total control of every area of your life . . . but you're entering into ME! You're giving Me your heart and allowing Me to replace it with My heart. Your will for My will. Your dreams—

My dreams for Your dreams.

Yes!

My weaknesses for Your strengths.

Yes!

Oh, Father! This is too good! I want it! I want it right now! Can I marry You right now, God?

Yes, My child.

I get it. I become whole and complete in You *first*. And later if You bring an earthly husband into my life—

Your marriage to Me will be the strongest foundation you can ever imagine for your earthly marriage.

Yes! Lord, I surrender. I mean . . . well, thanks that You've already forgiven my sins. And I'm grateful that You no longer hold them over me. But I realize now that You've only had a little of my heart. Right now, I kneel in absolute surrender to You. I want Your heart, Jesus. I want You to break me and remake me in Your image. I want to become one with You. I want You to empower me with YOU. I want to live and breathe and act and react Jesus, Jesus, Jesus!

I take you, My child.

I'm entering into a holy, eternal, intimate sacred marriage with the Creator of the universe!

Repeat after Me: On this day . . .

On this day . . .

. . . I willingly and obediently participate in an eternal marriage covenant with Jesus Christ, . . .

. . . I willingly and obediently participate in an eternal marriage covenant with Jesus Christ, . . .

. . . King of kings, . . .

. . . King of kings, . . .

. . . Lord of lords, . . .

. . . Lord of lords, . . .

. . . all-knowing Savior, . . .

. . . all-knowing Savior, . . .

. . . **and all-powerful God.**

. . . and all-powerful God.

I make this sacred oath realizing that I am pledging myself in total surrender . . .

I make this sacred oath realizing that I am pledging myself in total surrender . . .

. . . **for all eternity . . .**

. . . for all eternity . . .

. . . **to the control and authority of Jesus Christ.**

. . . to the control and authority of Jesus Christ.

I realize that He may someday bring a husband into my life, . . .

I realize that He may someday bring a husband into my life, . . .

. . . **but Jesus Christ will always be my first and foremost marriage partner.**

. . . but Jesus Christ will always be my first and foremost marriage partner.

If I am someday wedded to another person—

If I am someday wedded to another person—

. . . **under the direction of God Almighty—**

. . . under the direction of God Almighty—

. . . **that marriage will always take second place to my marriage with Jesus, . . .**

. . . that marriage will always take second place to my marriage with Jesus, . . .

. . . **and I will be careful to marry one who can only enhance my marriage to Christ—not detract from it.**

. . . and I will be careful to marry one who can only enhance my marriage to Christ—not detract from it.

Wow! Thank You, Father!

I love you.

And I love You back . . . with my *life!*

So . . . are *you* married? If you haven't become the Bride of Christ, right now would be a great time to walk down the aisle! Will you commit yourself totally to Him? When you marry the King of kings, you allow Him to begin molding and shaping your heart for your earthly husband.

On Keeping the Spiritual Fires Burning

God said: You're crying.

I said: Can't help it.

Want to talk about it?

I don't know.

I love talking with My children. Pick up your Bible.

Yeah?

And turn to Isaiah 1:18. What's it say?

"Come now, let us reason together."

That's fancy for "let's talk."

Hm. I like that. Give me another one.

Sure! Turn and read the second half of Isaiah 43:1.

"Fear not, for I have redeemed you; I have summoned you by name;
you are mine." Yeah. I like that a lot!

Let's go to the New Testament now. Find James 5:13, okay?

Okay. "Is any one of you in trouble? He should pray."

Again . . . *pray* is a pretty word for *talk*. Ready to talk? I'm more than ready to listen.

Yeah, I guess.

What is it, My child?

It's that mission trip I went on two weeks ago.

Yes?

Yeah. It was incredible, Father. I saw You work in so many ways.

Thank you for being willing to be used.

I'll never forget that trip.

I hope not. But I also hope it won't simply become a memory.

Whaddya mean? Of course it's a memory.

I want it to be more than that. I want it to become part of your lifestyle.

I want that too, God. And that's part of what's bugging me.

Go on.

I wanna live out everything I learned on the trip, but when I start talking about it, people don't seem all that interested.

Ah.

I mean, that trip was the greatest experience of my life! And it's like I can't even relate to people.

Hm. Let me try to help you understand.

Please do!

While you were on a mission trip in a different country for two weeks, your friends carried on with their lives.

Well, I know that.

No, think about it. Those two weeks have more or less become "frozen" for you. It's as if everything in your life stopped and re-organized itself for those two weeks.

Yeah, that's how I feel.

But your friends kept on doing chores, baby-sitting, working their part-time jobs, going out for pizza.

Yeah.

And they can't relate to what you've experienced.

But that's what's so frustrating! I *want* them to relate!

You had the privilege of experiencing what many people only dream of. They feel a little left out. You need to ask them about the last two weeks in *their* lives.

Why? You've already said they didn't do anything important. All they did was eat pizza and—

No, I never said what they did was unimportant. I said they kept doing what they usually do. They continued their daily routine.

Which really isn't that import—

Which is *very* important. Your Christian friends continued to serve and follow Me right here in their own element. You served and followed Me to another country. Both are equally important. When Jamie and Crystal went out for pizza, did you know they passed a woman on the street holding a sign?

No. What kind of sign?

"Will work for food."

Yeah, we see a lot of those.

But Jamie and Crystal did something about it.

What?

They purposely saved half the pizza they bought and took it to the woman on the street. She cried when they gave it to her.

Wow. I had no idea.

Because you didn't ask.

But I—

You assumed that what you were doing was far more important because you raised money all year to do it, and because you did it out of your comfort zone. And what you did *was* important! But you need to know that while you were holding Vacation Bible School for children who desperately needed it, Jamie was holding a baby with AIDS down at the shelter.

Wow.

You see, My child, as long as My disciples are truly committed to Me, I'll use them wherever they are.

I see that now. Thanks, God. I'll talk with You later. I wanna call Jamie and Crystal right now.

No, not yet.

How come?

Because you're not finished talking.

I'm not?

No. You're still hurting inside, aren't you?

How'd You know?

I'm God. I know. But I still want you to tell Me. It's part of praying. You don't pray to inform Me; you pray so that we can communicate.

Yeah, and I *want* to communicate with You. I so need that! I'd be lost without You, Father.

Keep on.

Well, I absolutely loved that mission trip. I've never experienced anything like it in my whole life! And I wanna share it with my friends. But when I whip out my photos, it's like they don't really get it, You know?

Well, part of the reason is because they'll never totally get it until they've experienced it themselves. Face it: They didn't smell Haiti. They have no idea what your supper tasted like—you're not even sure what it was!

That's for sure.

They didn't see the naked child with sores on her legs. They didn't hear the beating of pagan drums in the night. So until they actually experience it, is it really fair to expect them to get it?

No, I guess not. But I've got to share it!

And you will.

How?

With your life.

And how do I do that?

You *live out* the changes you've experienced.

Yes! That's exactly what I want, God! But I don't know how.

That's where I come in. I'll help you.

But what do I do?

While you were in Haiti, how much time were you spending with Me?

A bunch! I read my Bible in the morning before we left for ministry. And I read it every evening when we returned. It was like I couldn't get enough of it. I had to have it. I couldn't have done all I needed to do in Haiti without the strength that comes from Your Word.

And what about prayer?

Oh, remember God? I was praying all the time! It was like I was finally getting that verse that tells us to pray without ceasing.

Ephesians 6:18.

Yeah! That's the one. I never understood that before. I always thought, *Hey! That's impossible. How can anyone pray all the time?* But this summer I got it! I was able to set my mind in a framework of prayer that lasted throughout the day. I was constantly shooting up sentence prayers to You. And each evening, I couldn't wait to pour out my heart in prayer to You for all You'd done during the day. I was . . . I don't know . . . sort of really dependent on You.

That's it!

What?

You were totally dependent on Me. You realized you couldn't accomplish what I had called you to do in Haiti without My help.

So I depended on You.

And you drew strength from My Word.

And nourishment from my prayer times.

Exactly. And that needs to continue. I want you to be every bit as dependent on Me now as you were in Haiti.

But it seems different.

It *feels* different because you're not in a Third-World setting. You're not uncomfortable anymore. But to accomplish all I want to do through you at school and in your youth group, you still need My strength and My nourishment.

Yeah. I still need that total dependence on You.

That's right.

But what else?

Excuse Me?

A few minutes ago, You said *part* of the reason my friends don't get it is because they haven't experienced it.

Right.

What's the other part?

The other part is you.

Me? I'm not tracking with You, Lord.

Jamie and Crystal would have loved to participate on this mission trip. But Crystal's grandmother is in her last days, and Crystal's help is needed around home. Her mom is depending on her right now.

I know. And I'm so sorry about that.

And Jamie would have jumped at the chance to go to Haiti, but after her dad lost his employment, she began contributing money from her part-time job at the pet shop to her family's grocery needs.

Oh, man! I never knew that.

And when you presented your photos to them last week, you did it with a bit of an "air."

An air?

Think about it, My child. You were a little too proud. They picked up on your feeling of "I've been there, and you haven't. What I've done is more important than whatever you've been doing the last two weeks."

Ouch!

Double ouch.

I'm sorry, God. I really am. I love Jamie and Crystal. They're my best friends.

I know.

I don't wanna hurt them . . . but it sounds like I already have.

They understand that you've experienced something they haven't. And they're happy for your opportunity. In fact, they were praying for you every day you were gone. But they need to feel that what they were doing right here at home was just as important as what you were doing overseas.

Yeah, I understand now, Father. I need to apologize.

And you need to ask them about *them*.

I will.

And after they've talked about themselves for a while, and after a little more time has passed, you can get the photos out again.

Why? They don't understand.

You can help them. But do it the right way. Instead of shoving them under their noses and *telling* them, *share* with them. And instead of talking about the *trip*, talk about *specifics*—like the little girl with sores on her head. Relate it to them.

But *how* do I relate it to them?

Example: "This is Juanita. There are nine children in her family. That's why she doesn't have any clothes. They're too poor for each kid to have clothing. I loved holding her and rocking her to sleep one afternoon. Crystal, remember the time you held the sick baby in our church nursery? She'd just thrown up, and I didn't wanna get near her. But you reached out and cradled her in your arms. Remember how it felt to hold her and know you were doing the right thing? Well, that's how I felt when I rocked Juanita to sleep. It was cool—like in some small way I was making a tiny difference."

Oh.

I'll help you relate your experience to their lives.

Wow. The way You just said all that! It sounds so gentle, so inviting. I mean . . . if I were listening to You say that, I think I'd be going, "Show me the next picture. Tell me more!"

And that's how Jamie and Crystal—and the rest of your friends—will eventually react. But right now, you need to take it slow and concentrate on *their* feelings instead of *your* feelings.

What a dork I am, huh, God?

No, My child. You're human.

But You just keep loving me, don't You, God?

I sure do. And I'll never stop.

Can I go find Jamie and Crystal now?

I'll go with you.

On What Others Think

*E*ven though it's natural to want to look our best and be at our best, we reach a danger point when we become obsessed with those concerns. When we become more concerned with what others think than what God thinks, our priorities are messed up.

As you pray the next conversation, ask God to help you rearrange your priorities, if necessary, so that everything in your life revolves around Him and is in its proper balance.

God said: Okay, you've been in front of the mirror for forty-five minutes already.

I said: So?

So I wish you'd spend even half that time reading My Word.

But I've got to look my best, God. It's the first day of school!

There's nothing wrong with wanting to look your best—as long as it doesn't consume you.

Consume me?

Take up more of your time, thoughts, and energy than it should.

You're mad at me because I bought new blush?

No.

Lip gloss?

No.

Eyeliner.

No.

If it's not makeup, what is it?

Again, there's nothing wrong with wanting to look your best. A little makeup can enhance the natural beauty I've already given you. But you're becoming too concerned with what other people think.

That's crazy.

Is it?

Yes! I don't care what other people think!

So why'd you call Alexia three times this morning to ask what she's wearing?

Well . . . because, um . . .

And why'd you ignore Dustin two days ago when you picked up your class schedule?

Hey, he's weird, God! I couldn't be seen talking to *him*.

Why not?

Well, what would people think?

What'd you say?

AHHH! I can't believe I just said that.

I can. You've been thinking it for quite some time now.

Well, okay, maybe once with Dustin I was a little self-conscious about what students might think about me. But that's all.

And when Darci asked you to share a locker with her?

Well, God, that was ridiculous!

Why?

Because Darci doesn't really have any friends. And I've been waiting for two years to get to have a locker on the cool row. Now I finally have it!

Hm. What if you *had* agreed to share Darci's locker?

Huh! I couldn't do that—kids would think *I* didn't have friends either!

Who would think?

Kids. They'd think—

Um.

AHHHH! I can't believe I said that again.

Doesn't it get a little tiring always worrying about what others are thinking?

I never thought about it before.

Think about it: You're spending a lot of energy being too concerned about other people's reactions and opinions of you. Let's get this thing in perspective, okay?

How do I do that?

I'll help you. And as always, you can find guidance in My Word. So check out Isaiah 26:3.

I found it! "You will keep in perfect peace him whose mind is steadfast, because he trusts in you."

***Steadfast.* Know what it means?**

Not exactly.

It means you'll experience deep, settled peace when you turn your thoughts over and over and over again to Me.

So when I start worrying about what someone's thinking of me, what do I do?

Stop thinking about that person and start thinking about Me.
Talk to Me. Activate your prayer life—right then, right on the spot!
Hm.

Check out 1 John 2:15.

"So he made a whip out of cords—"

No, that's John 2:15. That's the Gospel of John. *First* John is toward the end of the Bible—right before Revelation.

Oh, yeah. I knew that. "Do not love the world or anything in the world. If anyone loves the world, the love of the Father is not in him."

What does that mean?

That I can't enjoy makeup and new clothes?

No. It's fun to dress up! And I understand your joy when you get a new pair of shoes. It's okay to like those things.

Then I don't get it.

It only becomes wrong when you enjoy *things* more than you enjoy Me.

I don't know *how* to enjoy You, God.

Get to know Me. The more you know Me, the more you'll understand Me. Turn in your Bible to Colossians 4:2.

Want me to read it out loud?

Yes, go ahead.

"Devote yourselves to prayer, being watchful and thankful."

When you truly devote yourself to Me, you'll automatically get to know Me better. And the more you know Me, the more I pour Myself into you.

And the more I'll quit worrying about what others think of me?

Exactly.

I don't *want* to worry, Lord. What I'd really like is to be free and secure and confident.

And you can be.

How? How do I become that?

You become confident and free and secure by strengthening your relationship with Me.

How does that help?

Since I created you, it stands to reason that I know you better than anyone else, right?

Yeah, that makes sense.

As your Creator, I *know* you better and *love* you more than anyone else in the entire world!

Yeah?

And if I already love you, that means you don't have to measure up. In other words—

I don't have to wear the right thing or look a certain way for You to accept me, cuz You already do!

Yes, My child. Yes! And when your security is founded on something that can't be destroyed, it will last.

What's my security in now?

It's in how you look. And in your friends. You've placed your security in a variety of things, but those things are all temporary.

Could You explain that?

Sure. Think about it this way: You could be in an accident and lose your looks in the blink of an eye.

I never thought of that.

And your friends? What if they all moved? Then where would your security be?

I don't know.

And your singing voice makes you feel secure, but if you lost your voice—

I get it; I wouldn't feel secure anymore.

Right. But when you place your security in Me, you're placing it in something eternal. Unshakable. Unswerving.

That's what I want, Father.

And when your security is truly grounded in Me, you won't be as concerned about what others are thinking.

How do I get that?

It comes from trusting Me.

And how do I learn to trust You?

By spending time with Me.

What'll we do? Just hang?

What do you do with your friends?

We hang. We talk. We read each other's e-mails.

We'll do the same: We'll hang out together. We'll talk with one another. And I want you to read My e-mail.

Your e-mail?

The Bible. It's My personal letter to you.

Oh, I get it!

It'll provide you with everything you need to establish a close, growing relationship with Me.

How do I know?

Read 2 Timothy 3:16.

New Testament, right?

Right.

Uh, here it is. "The whole Bible was given to us by inspiration from God and is useful to teach us what is true and to make us realize what is wrong in our lives; it straightens us out and helps us do what is right. It is God's way of making us well prepared at every point, fully equipped to do good to everyone" (TLB). Wow. I never knew that was in there.

There's a lot more where that came from!

I'm ready when You are, God.

Good.

So what do we do first?

I want you to call someone.

Jeremy? He looked so fine in his practice football jersey yesterday.

No, not Jeremy.

Who, then?

Darci.

But . . . people might think—I mean—um . . . yeah. I'll call her.

Do you know what to say?

I think I'll ask her to eat lunch with me in the cafeteria tomorrow at school.

I'm proud of you, My child.

And I'm already feeling more confident! Thanks, Father!

19

On Persecution

God said: We need to talk.

I said: I can't. It hurts too much.

I'm hurting with you.

I know You are, God. But that doesn't help right now.

My child, your reward will be great in heaven.

Yeah, I know. But it sure would feel good to get a reward right now. Heaven seems too far away to even imagine.

Since you don't feel like talking, I'll do the speaking, okay?

K.

And I'll do it through My Word.

K.

You've been reading in 2 Timothy.

Yeah. And it helps.

Good. Let's keep reading—together. Will you read 2 Timothy 3:1 to Me?

Sure. "You may as well know this too, Timothy, that in the last days it is going to be very difficult to be a Christian" (TLB). Wow. That's an understatement!

And let Me hear 2 Timothy 4:5.

K. "Stand steady, and don't be afraid of suffering for the Lord" (TLB). I'm not afraid, God. I'm just so hurt. And very, very tired.

I know. My child. And I understand. The world wasn't very kind to Me either. It hated Me, and it will hate you because you love Me.

I know that. I've always been taught that. So why is it always so hard?

Knowing and experiencing are two different things. But remember, My child, there's nothing you'll experience that I won't go through with you.

I think I'm ready to talk now.

Good.

It was after school—we'd finished basketball practice—and we were all in the locker room. Ashley was bragging about going all the way with Bryce. And Hannah was talking about what a great kisser Nathan is. And then everyone started in. They were all talking about sex and their guys, and I guess someone realized I wasn't saying anything. And Ashley goes, "So come on! Don't keep secrets. Tell us about *your* Friday nights."

Go on.

Well, I just stood there. My heart was beating really fast. Then Hannah goes, "Yeah, who's the latest guy *you've* done it with?"

It's okay to cry.

But I don't wanna cry! I'm tired of crying. Ugh! I can't help it. Here I am, crying again!

Go on.

So I said, "I haven't been with a guy." And Sheree goes, "What do you mean?" So I said I was a virgin.

I'm proud of you.

And they laughed. Hannah couldn't believe it. Tiffany goes, "But that's impossible—you're in high school!"

I know.

So I said, "Yeah, I'm a virgin. I've decided not to have sex until I'm married." And Ashley goes, "So . . . you're gay?" Then Sheree's all, "I knew there was something weird about her!" And Hannah's going, "That's sick! We havta share our locker room with her!"

I'm so sorry.

I wish I'd quit crying.

It's okay. Go on.

Well, I tried to explain that I'm saving sex until marriage not because I'm gay but because I'm a Christian and I want God's best. But I don't think they heard me.

Some of them did.

And Ashley ran outta the locker room with Hannah on her heels. They were telling everyone, God! I wanted to run. I wanted to hide! I wanted to die.

You're being persecuted, My child.

Now Ashley and Hannah are spreading this rumor that I'm gay. God, it hurts so bad!

And you'll be blessed because of your persecution. Read it, okay? Matthew 5:10.

"Blessed are those who are persecuted because of righteousness, for theirs is the kingdom of heaven."

Do you trust Me?

Yes, Lord, I do. I really, really do. And I wouldn't change my answer for anything. I'm committed to You. I've surrendered all. You know that.

Yes, I do know that. Let's read 1 Timothy 3:16.

K. "It is quite true that the way to live a godly life is not an easy matter. But the answer lies in Christ" (TLB). Yeah. I know that, Jesus.

Without Your strength, I wouldn't make it. You're the only reason I made it through the day.

Check out 1 Peter 2:11. You've already got it underlined.

Yeah. I'll try to memorize it. This is a good one! "Dear friends, I urge you, as aliens and strangers in the world, to abstain from sinful desires, which war against your soul."

Aliens and strangers in this world. You're only a visitor here, My child. This is simply your temporary dwelling place. Your real home is not of this earth. Your real place is with Me. Remember that.

Yeah. I will, Jesus. I long for heaven! I can't wait to get to be with You forever.

Keep reading. 1 Peter 2:12.

"Live such good lives among the pagans that, though they accuse you of doing wrong, they may see your good deeds and glorify God on the day he visits us." I will, Lord. With You living through me, I *will* continue on. I can't do it in my own strength, but I'll keep my commitment to holiness.

I won't show you the future right now, My child. But I want you to know that Jennifer and Meredith heard what you said.

What?

When Ashley and Hannah were running out of the locker room and spreading lies about you, Jennifer and Meredith heard you say that you're not gay and that you're a Christian.

They did?

Yes.

What does that mean?

It's not time to reveal these things to you, My child. But know . . . and trust . . . that you planted some powerful seeds.

I did?

Yes, My child! Powerful, potent seeds of hope and righteousness.

Wow!

Yes!

That makes the pain not hurt so bad.

Great will be your reward, My child. You'll not cry one single tear that I don't cry with you.

Thank You, God. Thank You! Continue to strengthen me. I want nothing more than to be all You call me to be.

I love you, My child.

And I love You, Lord.

You may never be beaten to death for your faith in God, but you may be persecuted in other ways—being ignored, cut down, mocked, cursed at, or made fun of by teachers or professors who don't share your faith. God never promised us an easy life; He *did* promise that He'd be faithful, that He would never leave us.

Right now would be a great time to pray for Christians who are being persecuted by much more than mockery. For Christians around the world who are being physically tortured and killed because of their faith, ask for God's comfort and strength.

Also, ask God what you can do to help make your own church aware of persecuted Christians. Talk with your pastor about planning a service around this idea. And check out the information on the persecuted church at: www.persecutedchurch.org.

About the Author

*S*usie Shellenberger is the editor of *Brio* magazine, Focus on the Family's monthly publication for teen girls. Susie's a former high-school drama teacher and youth pastor. She also co-hosts Focus on the Family's weekly talk-radio show for teens: *Life on the Edge: Live!* Susie has written twenty-eight books and travels as a national speaker.

If you'd like information on scheduling Susie to speak for your youth or women's event, contact The Ambassador Agency at 615-377-9100. If you'd like a complimentary copy of *Brio* magazine, call 1-800-232-6459. If you'd like to know whether *Life on the Edge: Live!* is broadcast in your area, call 1-800-232-6459.